SHAME AND HUMILIATION

PSYCHOANALYTIC IDEAS AND APPLICATIONS SERIES

IPA Publications Committee

Gennaro Saragnano (Rome), Chair; Leticia Glocer Fiorini (Buenos Aires), Consultant; Samuel Arbiser (Buenos Aires); Catalina Bronstein (London); Paulo Cesar Sandler (São Paulo); Christian Seulin (Lyon); Mary Kay O'Neil (Montreal); Gail S. Reed (New York); Rhoda Bawdekar (London), Ex-officio as Publications Officer

Other titles in the Series

SHAME AND HUMILIATION

A Dialogue between Psychoanalytic and Systemic Practices

*Carlos Guillermo Bigliani,
Rodolfo Moguillansky,
and Carlos E. Sluzki*

General Editor

Gennaro Saragnano

KARNAC

First published in 2013 by
Karnac Books Ltd
118 Finchley Road, London NW3 5HT

British Library Cataloguing in Publication Data

A C.I.P. for this book is available from the British Library

ISBN 978 1 78220 029 1

Edited, designed and produced by The Studio Publishing Services Ltd
www.publishingservicesuk.co.uk
e-mail: studio@publishingservicesuk.co.uk

Printed in Great Britain

www.karnacbooks.com

CONTENTS

PSYCHOANALYTIC IDEAS AND APPLICATIONS SERIES

IPA Publications Committee

The Publications Committee of the International Psychoanalytical Association continues, with this volume, the series "Psychoanalytic Ideas and Applications".

The aim of this series is to focus on the scientific production of significant authors whose works are outstanding contributions to the development of the psychoanalytic field and to set out relevant ideas and themes, generated during the history of psychoanalysis, that deserve to be known and discussed by present psychoanalysts.

The relationship between psychoanalytic ideas and their applications has to be put forward from the perspective of theory, clinical practice, technique, and research so as to maintain their validity for contemporary psychoanalysis.

The Publication Committee's objective is to share these ideas with the psychoanalytic community and with professionals in other related disciplines, in order to expand their knowledge and generate a productive interchange between the text and the reader.

It is, then, with great pleasure that I am presenting now this new volume on *Shame and Humiliation*, authored by Carlos Guillermo Bigliani, Rodolfo Moguillansky, and Carlos E. Sluzki. The book is organised in a way that allows the reader to listen to a dialogue between different theoretical approaches: psychoanalysis and systemic theory. In my opinion, the format is an original and intelligent one (three authors who discuss the topics in a quite dynamic way from different points of view, trying to integrate them), and I think it could be rather useful to many different types or readers. Besides, there is one further point that I, as the Series Editor, would like to stress. It has always been one of IPA's main objectives to deal with the fundamental issue of Outreach. As contemporary psychoanalysts, I think we have to try to dialogue with other related disciplines, in order to let psychoanalysis be known and considered by a wider public. It is my conviction that this book, *Shame and Humiliation*, is a useful and viable way to face this fundamental issue.

Gennaro Saragnano
Series Editor
Chair, IPA Publications Committee

Carlos Guillermo Bigliani, MD, is a psychiatrist and psychoanalyst, a former member of the research department at the G. A. Alfaro General Hospital in Lanus, Buenos Aires (under the direction of Mauricio Goldenberg), a researcher and professor in the department of occupational medicine (University of Buenos Aires Medical School), professor of the Seminar on Neuroses (University of Buenos Aires School of Psychology), professor of Psychoanalysis at the Sedes Sapientiae Post-Graduate Institute (São Paulo, Brazil), and professor of Psychoanalytic Psychopathology and Family Therapy at the Pontificia Universidade Catolica (São Paulo, Brazil). He has published articles in numerous professional journals and also contributed chapters in books, including "Freud: Jewish culture and modernity", which was awarded the Jabuti Prize in Brazil. He is a member of the Buenos Aires Psychoanalytic Association (a member of the International Psychoanalytic Association), the International Association of Couple and Family Psychoanalysis, and board member of the Human Dignity and Humiliation Studies Organization and other professional organisations. He is invited professor of Family Therapy in the University of São Paulo and co-ordinator of the Berggasse 19 Centre in São Paulo, Brazil.

Rodolfo Moguillansky, MD, is a psychiatrist and psychoanalyst, Rector of Buenos Aires Institute of Mental Health, and professor at the Buenos Aires Institute of Mental Health and in the department of mental health, University of Buenos Aires Medical School. He has been a guest lecturer at different universities, including the Universidade do São Paulo (Brazil), the Universidad Complutense (Madrid, Spain), the Universidad de Santiago de Compostela (Spain), and the Universidad del Valle de Cali (Colombia). He is a full member of the Buenos Aires Psychoanalytic Association, the International Psychoanalytic Association, and the International Federation of Psychotherapy Associations. He has published articles in Spanish, Portuguese, Italian, and English and is the author, co-author, and compiler of more than twenty books. He has been awarded the Bleger (1998) and Storni (2000) prizes by the Argentine Psychoanalytic Association, the Liberman prize (1999), by the Buenos Aires Psychoanalytic Association, and the FEAP prize (2008) by the Spanish Federation of Psychotherapy Associations.

Carlos E. Sluzki, MD, was trained in psychiatry in the department of psychopathology, G. A. Alfaro General Hospital in Lanus (Argentina) under the leadership of Dr Mauricio Goldenberg, in psychoanalysis at the Argentine Psychoanalytic Association, and in family therapy at the Mental Research Institute (Palo Alto, California), where he was research associate (1965–1976), director of training (1976–1980), and director (1980–1983). He has been professor of psychiatry at the Universities of San Francisco and Los Angeles, California, as well as at the University of Massachusetts Medical School; editor-in-chief of the journals *Acta Psiquiátrica y Psicológica de América Latina* (1967–1971), *Family Process* (1983–1988), and *American Journal of Orthopsychiatry* (1992–1998), and an adviser to the World Health Organisation, the United Nations High Commission on Refugees, and the Office of the Prosecutor of the International Criminal Court. He is currently a professor in the department of global and community health and at the School for Conflict Analysis and Resolution, at George Mason University, Arlington, Virginia, and clinical professor of psychiatry and behavioural sciences at George Washington University, in Washington, DC. He has published over 200 professional articles and books, and is an honorary member of numerous professional organisations in Europe, Asia, and the Americas.

PROLOGUE

Shame and Humiliation aims at exploring a sub-set of universal emotions, emotions labelled as "negative" because the dis-ease they generate when we experience them and the tenacity with which we try to avoid them, thus becoming a powerful instrument in the power "games" of our species, making their mark in well intentioned education as well as in merciless relations of oppression. Universal as they might be, though, these emotions are triggered by, experienced, and displayed in varied ways according to the mandates of different cultures (Should I blush in silence or unsheath my knife and take revenge?) and the vicissitudes of different socio-cultural strata (Should I lower my gaze or react with contempt?).

The first subjective inkling of these emotions tend to appear very early in our upbringing process. In fact, triggering shame and humiliation, or the threat of so doing, are used abundantly in the socialising process of infants, a period in which we learn, whether we like it or not, about the oppressive power of the opinion of the Meaningful Others, quickly incorporated as one of the important determinants of our self-perception. In that sense, our self-esteem is partly a prisoner of the appreciation or depreciation that we attribute to those with whom we interact (modified by many other variables, among which is how much we appreciate their opinion). They, in turn, might feel they are partially prisoners of their perception of our value judgements towards them, and so on, in an endless gallery of mirrors. We say "partially prisoner" since those early experiences usually leave their mark as a tendency towards one or another bias in our self-perception, making us more or less vulnerable in the long run to opinions expressed by Others or attributed to them and, even more problematic, to our opinion of ourselves, and skewed towards one or another of these emotions.

Shame and humiliation are *private emotions*, experienced within our innermost intimate being. We sometimes detect them clearly in our field of accessible emotions, but sometimes they express themselves in our demeanour or our behaviour, even before we become aware of them. They are emotions which we might try to hide, as if it would be wrong to feel them, or we might fully display them, as if it were a matter of honour, or we might even say manliness, though it would be politically and factually incorrect, as these emotions appear in both genders with similar intensity, although sometimes triggered by different circumstances.

But shame and humiliation are also *social emotions*, as they arise and are displayed in interpersonal situations, in narratives with three main characters—perpetrators (sometimes us, sometimes the others), victims (same comment), and witnesses (external or internal, gentle or cruel). The latter are sometimes comprehensive ("The public eye"), sometimes fully known to us ("What will Mother say!"), sometimes multitudinous (our friends, our enemies), and, on occasions, ghostlike ("What if somebody saw me!"). They might echo our personal history ("I felt like I was five years old again!), and project into the future ("I will never be able to look him in the face again!").

The plots of the narratives embedding those emotions are paradigmatic, so much so that most fairy tales as well as major literary works—which are supported by, and remind us of, social instructions about good and evil, about behaviours to be rewarded and punished—have one or the other of these emotions as a leitmotiv.

Shame and humiliation are two compasses that help to orientate our behaviour as social beings, guided by a shared code that allows us to live our life as part of a society (and a culture), reminding us of what is permitted and what is forbidden, what is accepted and what is rejected. In fact, we describe an antisocial individual as "shame-less", as if the lack of the feeling would imply something alien to what is essentially human.

While *shame* is a feeling that prompts us to want to hide or escape, even to kill ourselves so as to wash it away from us, *humiliation*, in its narrative of unfairness, unleashes intense levels of passion that, as we know, favours violent actions, revenge, and "vendettas", and which is offered to justify murders, kidnappings, the madness of wars, and many other atrocities. In spite of their ubiquity, their omnipresence, their simultaneously universal and intimate nature, hidden as well as socially enacted, the "psy" world seems to have shown a certain reticence in exploring them. At the very least, we can say that "shame and humiliation" has not yet enjoyed its fifteen minutes of fame. We hope that this book will both contribute to, and encourage, a more thorough exploration of these emotions.

How did this joint book project of ours come about? It started when we decided, in a corridor conversation at a congress in which we were chatting about the challenge of discussing core themes from conceptual vantage points that were discontinuous, to put that challenge to test by organising a two-day workshop with the title "Humillaçao e vergonha: um dialogo psicoanalitico–sistêmico" [Humiliation and shame: a psychoanalytic–systemic dialogue]. That adventure took place, in fact, in São Paulo, Brazil in April 2008. At the workshop, each of the three of us delivered a plenary presentation, followed by discussions by the other two, followed in turn by stimulating exchanges that included the participation of several distinguished colleagues as well as that of an enthusiastic professional audience.

But, more prehistorically, what connects us as a trio to start with had been a relationship of mutual affection and friendship of long standing, and a trajectory which goes back to our shared experience in the Department of Psychopathology at the former Policlinico G. Araoz Alfaro, now called Hospital Zonal 'Evita', in Lanus, a suburb of Buenos Aires. That department, headed by *avant-garde* psychiatrist Dr Mauricio Goldenberg, to whom many professionals, including the three authors, are deeply indebted, acquired great prestige and exerted a major ideological influence on the training of psychiatrists and psychologists in the sixties and into the seventies.[1] This influence was to wane, as happened with many other institutions during the dark times of a harsh military dictatorship that gripped Argentina in the late 1970s.

Our relationship, which began in that educational context (Sluzki being the young professor of the other two authors, even younger residents at that time!), turned into a friendship which has lasted through the years even though our itinerant lifestyle, caused partly by political circumstances and partly by professional interests, kept us geographically apart. In fact, one of us (RM) lives in Argentina, another (CGB) in Brazil, and the third (CS), in the USA.

The three of us completed our psychoanalytical training in Argentina. However, our common interest in interpersonal processes followed different paths. CS, involved since early in his career in social psychiatric research, focused his interest on interpersonal dynamics and, as an extension, on family therapy, and incorporated into his view what were initially called "cybernetic" and then "systemic" models for their understanding. GB and RM worked mostly on sharpening the focus of the psychoanalytical lens, a perspective from which they contributed to the understanding of family dynamics and culture, through both teaching and theory building.

It was precisely this relative divergence of approaches, against the backdrop of our friendship, which inspired us to explore the potential bridges that connect our viewpoints, putting to the test the coherence of our approaches as well as combining components of these alternative models, and to do so in public, as an additional challenge. Both our conceptual models and our affection and respect for each other, we are convinced, survived and were enriched by the challenge.

In preparing this book, we sent each other early drafts of our respective chapters and commented on them fairly frequently, making use of each other's opinions to refine our own contributions. This led to some very gratifying exchanges as well as an unexpected complication, which was that, to a certain extent, this process of writing and rewriting, and re-elaborating some components of our chapters on the basis of others' suggestions blurred the edges that had delineated our viewpoints. In fact, in the final manuscript, some subjects which at the beginning had triggered critical discussions ended up being reshaped and further elaborated to the point where they smoothed over some of the sharp borders between our viewpoints. So it happened that, in the process of writing this book, we achieved what we had defined as one of our objectives: the building of conceptual bridges.

We hope that, with this contribution to the vast subject of shame and humiliation, we have been able to answer some potential questions, and, needless to say, to generate many others, clarifying some possible doubts and introducing new ones, as a contribution to that endless dialectical cycle that characterises the process of knowledge building.

Carlos Guillermo Bigliani, São Paulo, Brazil
Rodolfo Moguillansky, Buenos Aires, Argentina
Carlos E. Sluzki, Washington DC, USA

Note

1.   For a detailed discussion of the impact of this programme and of its director in the development of the field of mental health in Argentina, see, among others, Visacovsky (2002) and Wolfson (2009).

CHAPTER ONE

Humiliation and shame: dynamics and destinies

Carlos Guillermo Bigliani

By way of an introduction: psychoanalytical and systemic approaches

This book and the meeting from which it originated represent an effort to build bridges between the different ways, both psychoanalytical and systemic, of thinking about the subject and its context, which can cross-fertilise each other. This requires an approach that does not treat the models as if they were religious dogma.

Freud had a mature relationship with his theories, going so far as to call his metapsychology (a name given to his theorisations over clinics) "our mythology". Freud suggested to Ferenczi, a brilliant Hungarian analyst, that "you should not theorize. Theories should come to you unexpectedly, like an uninvited stranger" (Gribinski, 1994, p. 1013). But once the stranger comes in, he reorganises our perception. Winnicott says, "when I do my clinical work, I produce theories for my own good, and they have an influence on what I see and hear, as well as on what I do" (Winnicott, 1971, p. 20).

Blum remembers that in the 1930s, the mainstream of psychoanalytical thinking had taken refuge in the theorisation of the intrapsychic and held the opinion that "any menace which threatened the (theoretical) importance of psychic reality was risking the sound-ness and security of the psychoanalytical movement" (Blum, 1994, p. 872). Even though Freud himself had already proposed that, in order to overcome the obstacles he had had to face owing to his limitations in the treatment of psychoses, the explanatory theory should be expanded and the technique should be changed (Freud, 1916–1917).

Some authors argue that taking refuge in the intrapsychic was an effect of the self-limitation that appeared in the theory owing to the repressive atmosphere of Nazism in the culture. Several authors describe the way in which this climate was infiltrating the life of German and Austrian psychoanalytical institutions, often with the alleged pretext of saving those institutions: the psychoanalyst candidates were reprimanded if they developed social or political activities opposed to the regime, and Jewish analysts were asked to resign their membership of certain professional societies whose directors were non-Jewish. (In fact, a psychiatrist who was a relative of Field-Marshal Goering was appointed president of the Psychoanalytical Association in Berlin, in order to protect the future of the institution (Bigliani, 2003, p. 180).) This oppressive climate weighing on the German analysts, many of them socialist-minded (and who, soon after migrating to the USA, would face the repressive atmosphere of McCarthyism) might have contributed, according to these interpretations, to a "pasteurisation" of the theory, proposing "conflict-free areas" with no contact with external reality, in the developments of ego psychology (Langer, 1981, p. 64).

With this in mind, Blum reminds us that the publication of Ferenczi's famous article, "The confusion of tongues between adults and the child", in which he anticipated concepts about accumulative trauma and the notion of a child's self-censorship, guilt, and shame resulting from child abuse, was banned until Balint, his former patient and admirer, authorised publication almost twenty years later (Blum, 1994, p. 874). As Blum points out in his article, the ban was related to the requirement of the psychoanalytic mainstream to approach the search for the causes of pathologies in the interior of the mind. As Freud had already done some time before, when he abandoned the seduction theory,[1] a chapter in this return to the interior, denying interpersonal causality, was being rewritten. This attitude towards theory favoured the appearance—about fifty years ago and in various places—of a feeling of dissatisfaction towards the predominant tendencies in schools of psychodynamic psychology which were especially interested in the intrapsychic, and whose results were considered by many to be unsatisfactory. Perhaps also as a reaction against this excessive appreciation of the intrapsychic, in the early 1950s there was a strengthening of a pragmatic and creative conception that emphasised analysis of interactions and the systems of which subjects were parts as principal determinants of psychopathology, leaving aside intrapsychical determinations. The latter remained as if in a "black box", whose mechanisms were not unknown to most of the original authors, but who, nevertheless, chose to exclude them from their theorisation. Don D. Jackson, as well as Salvador Minuchin, Nathan Ackerman, Lyman C. Wynne, Theodore Lidz, Israel Zwerling, Ivan Boszormengi-Nagy, Carl Whittaker, Carlos Sluzki, and many of the other first family therapists who participated in this movement in the USA came from psychoanalytical training, whereupon their roads diverged (Nichols & Schwartz, 2007, p. 213). They considered that many reflections about the intrapsychic were paralysing and unproductive, and they thought that freedom from the hindrance of psychodynamisms and their interpretation lent consistency to their crusade in favour of a new theory and therapeutic practice.

That movement caused many therapists to cast aside "the interior of the mind" and devote themselves to the study of the systems of relationships in which patients are immersed, and of the mechanisms that made the system sick and would, in turn, make the patients sick. They also studied those relationships from an interactive perspective, proposing models such as the "double bind" (Bateson, Jackson, Haley, & Weakland, 1956; Watzlawick, Beavin, & Jackson, 1967) and forms of paradoxical communication as "efficient ways" to cause illness (Sluzki & Ransom, 1976). These constitute the basic explorations of systemic thinking and inform the understanding of most therapists in their clinical work with families.

This movement broadened and enriched our critical outlook as therapists on intrapsychic reductionism, and some of its authors produced wonderful articles about what constitutes the worst of psychoanalysis and its transferential abuses (e.g., Haley, 1969). But some of them threw away the intrapsychic baby together with the bathwater of poor-quality psychoanalysis.

Several psychoanalytical authors also pointed out the importance of culture, society, family, and the "Other" in creating the subject and his pathology, in a way distancing themselves from what is strictly intrapsychic to enter the field of what was being developed by the theoretical movement described above. In addition to Freud, with his profound reflections on the masses, culture, and history, other noted authors followed that path. It is worth mentioning among them Lacan, who took up the Freudian concept with regard to the construction of a subject in which the presence of the "Other" was essential, his theorisations about the family, and his descriptions of the functions or places of the characters that make up its whole, Bion, when theorising on the capacity of maternal reverie as a foundation for the production of symbols, and Aulagnier with her thinking about subjectivity based on the anticipated meeting of a mother with her unborn child.[2]

Research into the use of the concept of paradox, frequent during the period when the systemic movement was being developed, especially by the team formed by Selvini Palazzoli, Boscolo, Cecchin, and Prata (1974), also found significant developments, but in an intrapsychic dimension among psychoanalysts who treated serious pathologies. Rousillon (1995, p. 11) goes so far as to consider that just as the conflict would be the axis along which the field of neuroses lines up, the paradox would be the axis illuminating the comprehension of narcissistic affections. He describes how several authors, for example Winnicott and Bion, showed the existence of defences he calls "paradoxical", destined to fight against traumas wrongly symbolised in the past, that would come to be expressed as a paradoxical fear that what had happened in the past might really happen in the future. Thus, suicide would be a paradoxical defence in the face of a psychic death that had previously occurred, and anorexia a paradoxical defence in the face of an existing ailment produced by an internal emptiness, or an attack on the link would be a paradoxical defence in the face of a lost link. Rousillon suggests that the task of the analyst would be to transform these experiences (which have not reached the symbolic level) into thoughts.

I believe that when therapists work in this zone of psychopathology, given its clinical implications, they must bear in mind both intrapsychic paradoxality and communicational paradoxes of the family system. "Paradoxality", then, circumscribes an area of confluences where psychoanalytical and systemic contributions complement each other.

Other areas of development and of approximation/confrontation between systemic and psychoanalytical thinking should include a reflection on "actuality" (and history) of the determinant phenomena of pathology and on the "widening scope" of the field from which the theoretical approach explains the phenomena to be analysed, that is, a discussion that would include an analysis of the determinant "sets" in the production of subjects and/or pathologies.

In other words, if what is dominant for each discipline in this production would be foetal relationships, the mother's unconscious, early relationships with both parents, the current dynamics of the family, if the subject (or his pathology) reflects his times and his culture more than his family, etc.

In recent decades, systemic therapists' effort to focus on the actuality of the system has found a parallel in the psychoanalytical field. Some theorisers came to reassess—within the whole of determinants of mental pathology (complementary series)—the variables linked to current determinants, thus expanding the field of determination.

Berenstein, for instance, questions the therapeutic efficacy of interpreting "the repetition of the past in transference" in some cases of negative therapeutic reaction. According to classic psychoanalytical theory, that past would be represented in the present of the relationship with the therapist (transference) and this relationship should always be the axis of intervention. This author suggests that this kind of interpretation in some of those cases can be not only useless, but even iatrogenic, and contribute to stereotyping the patient in his repetition. He proposes, instead, an understanding of the importance of the fact, of what is current, what is new, and of the effect of the presence of the other to stimulate change and build the bond.

> According to psychoanalysis, symptoms became intelligible when they were set in the context of the mental structure of the person suffering; if they are considered within the family structure they will acquire a greater degree of intelligibility and even more if they are included in their social background ... Every sign acquires a qualitatively greater degree of intelligibility when it is included in a wider context. (Berenstein, 2007, p. 39, translated for this edition)

Several authors, including Berenstein, Puget, and Kaës, propose a mental apparatus arranged in terms of a linking structure that would unfold in the intrasubjective, intersubjective, and trans-subjective spaces, with the corresponding unconscious of each space. "The three spaces—internal world, world of links, and socio-cultural world—are distinct, differentiated, and are linked in the subject, who, in turn, is their product. Each one of these spaces produces an unconscious" (Berenstein, 2004, p. 142, translated for this edition).

The unconscious of the *intrasubjective world* is made up of the articulation of repressed representations and affects according to current classic topology.

The *relational* or *intersubjective world* produces its unconscious with what both subjects will have to *suppress* or leave out, that which is not compatible with the relationship or what appears to them as alien.

> In the work of subjectivation, always pertinent to the relationship with another or with others, a new sense can be produced, since the link creates its own unconscious. A new sense corresponds to a new subjectivity. It will be said that the subject is "another" for others and "another" for himself. (Berenstein, 2004, p. 142, translated for this edition)

Finally, the unconscious of the social-cultural world, or trans-subjective space, will be instituted starting from that which ought to be suppressed or excluded from what is determined by the belonging of the subjects to the social group, including "the feelings of uncertainty in the face of the threats presented by the dissolution of the group" (Berenstein, 2004, p. 142, translated for this edition).

Kaës, along the same lines, says,

> The development of research on the transmission of psychic life through the new psychoanalytical devices implies a new model of intelligibility of the formation of the mental apparatus and of its articulation between the subjects of the unconscious. This research criticises the strictly intradetermined conceptions of the formation of the mental apparatus and the solipsistic formations of the individual. (Kaës, 1998b, p. 18, translated for this edition)

This allows us to imagine a subject who is not only constructed by his established identifications, but also by the acts of imposition permanently performed on him by others, with whom there will be mutual inducements, a multiple subject (different with each of the different others) who would participate in unconscious alliances, in denial pacts.

In this world of links, resistances due to complementary repetitions might appear that may be reciprocally strengthened in a bond that might be pathogenic (which would add up, in their overdetermination, to the intrapsychic resistances classically described by psychoanalysis), bonding structures of segregative or melancholic repetitions. In the same theoretical space, several authors have also worked on the question of the transmission of psychism between generations (see Abraham & Torok, 1978; Eiguer, 1983).

Parameters for considering humiliation: trans-subjectivity, trans-generationality

The feelings of humiliation and shame share an early fixation, a sensation of collapse of the ego, and a feeling of critical detachment from the internal judgemental instances of the subject.

It is necessary to differentiate the action of humiliation from the feeling of humiliation. The action appears often in the context of intolerance before what is different, of the extermination of that which is different.

To be humiliated (and feeling there is no way out) can favour the fixed idea or the act of suicide in subjects without major narcissistic fixations. The following account illustrates the point.

The history of Jews in Central Europe has been one of countless humiliations, expulsions, plundering, and massacres. They paid taxes to be able to live in Vienna as foreigners and, in spite of having lived in the city for centuries, they were subjected to a special branch of the police, who were present even at their weddings. The official documents addressed to them began like this: The Jew So-and-So (Bigliani & Dines, 2001).

In 1867, the Jews in the Austro-Hungarian Empire were emancipated,[3] which implied a great advance considering that, in 1777, less than a hundred years before, Empress Maria Theresa of Austria announced to the entire world that in the future no Jew ("as they are called") could enter Vienna without a permit written and signed by her. And she went on to say there was not any public plague worse than "those people", proposing that they should be kept apart and avoided as much as possible (Bigliani & Dines, 2001).

In this context, it is understandable that the great-grandfather of the main subject of our story required a permit to stay in a town. In a document still in existence, we read, "I appoint my grandson Jacob my companion . . . with this purpose I obtained the enclosed passports. For this reason I request that the Magistrate deign to grant me an Authorization to stay in Freiberg". The document, signed in 1844 by his great-grandfather, Ephraim, was required at the time because Jews without a passport or an authorisation were expelled even if they were regular residents of the country.

Years later, Schlomo, son of Jacob and great-grandson of Ephraim, tells us,

> To demonstrate that I had been born in much better times, my father told me the following story: "On a Saturday I went for a walk, well-dressed, along the streets of the city where you were born, and a Christian pulled off my hat, threw it into the mud and shouted—Jew! Get off the pavement!" to which Schlomo asked, "And what did you do, Father?" His father answered, "I took the hat out of the mud." I didn't think my father's behaviour was very heroic. (Freud, 1900a)

Apparently, times improved because, as his children say (see Jones, 1957), in 1901 Schlomo used his walking stick to confront a group of ten men and several women who were hurling anti-Semitic insults at him.

But the good times would not last long. A few decades later, in 1938, Schlomo discussed with his daughter Anna the advantages of suicide when the Nazi troops invaded Austria. In those times, when the suicide rate had increased by 500% in their city, Schlomo (the reader must have realised by now that I am referring to Sigmund Freud) and Anna (his daughter, Anna Freud) decided that committing suicide was what the Nazis wanted them to do (Figure 1.1).

Puget and colleagues remind us that social insertion is imposed upon the subject, and includes him in a history that precedes and succeeds him, pointing out the unconscious quality of the insertion, which transforms the subject into a transmitter and an actor of a social organisation in which he is both active and passive (Puget, de Bianchedi, Bianchedi, Braun, & Pelento, 1993). Kaës (1998b, p. 16) points out as well that "The question of the subject is increasingly defined in the intersubjective space, and more precisely in the space and the time of the generation of family and group".

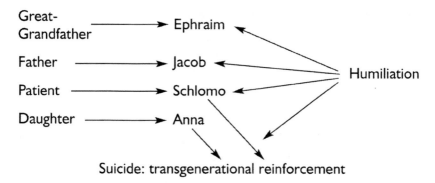

Figure 1.1. The possible transgenerational effects of humiliation.

The question of the precedence of the other, or more than one other, in the destiny of an individual persists as a challenge to understanding psychic life, where the ego can create itself or has difficulties in doing so. Kaës (1998a) refers to all the texts where Freud develops his great concern about the question of transmission between generations (*Totem and Taboo*, "Narcissism: an introduction", "Psychology of the masses", etc.) and proposes that the central characteristic "of these objects of transmission is that they are marked as negative". What is transmitted is that which we cannot hold, which is not retained, which we do not remember: things lacking, illnesses, shame, that which we repress, lost objects still mourned. Eiguer (1983, p. 33) states,

> what has not been said or has been poorly said produces family symptoms, and the picture of the ancestor appears as one "other" of our father . . . establishing a continuity between the source of descendance and the youngest representative. This object of transmission of psychic life between generations is disclosed as a messenger of kinship, of culture, and of law.

Thus, the repeated experiences of humiliation to which an adolescent might be subjected have the power to facilitate his conversion into a subject capable of committing collective crimes at school, or into a suicidal case, in the same way as experiences of humiliation of a people possibly facilitate the production of suicide bombers. In the case we are trying to exemplify, we can put forward the notion that transgenerational humiliations can facilitate the suicidal idea as an answer to a situation perceived as inescapable (and even have an influence on the appraisal of the situation). Fortunately, Freud chose a different road.

From the macro- to the microsocial

Enríquez, in his book *Da horda au estado* (From the Horde to the State) (1999, p. 320), stresses that the extermination of the Jews by the Nazi state is not only a sad accident of history, but it also constitutes a revealing element of the essence of modern states, an anticipatory image of more recent genocides as well as future genocides which the modern state will produce.[4]

In his work on anti-Semitism, Enríquez stresses that the Nazi state offered a model of how the modern state suffers from an inability to acknowledge "otherness", particularly in the case he studied. This was the otherness of a people who would not be assimilated, who would not be subjected to the state or to the official religion.

In his analysis of German history, Enríquez shows how the feudal states that divided the land managed to unite to form the German state after many vicissitudes on the way to realising a dream of unity as a nation, with one people sharing one race, one language, one religion, and one mythology. The state stumbled on an obstacle, the German Jewish people, an obstacle to being one in the face of the otherness, or the difference, that this people represented. For this reason they subjected the Jews to harassment and humiliation, which were preliminary to extermination, to the expulsion of what was different, and this "different" was weighed down with all the projections of their own frightful impurities (Figure 1.2).

Thus, the modern state would present a demand for uniformity in its task of creating a reality and in an attempt to dominate and exert control over the population. Undoubtedly, writers and artists anticipated the social effects of that uniformity or the delusional characteristics of the leader of the state, as in Charlie Chaplin's films *Modern Times* and *The Great Dictator*.

Lidia Jorge, an award-winning Portuguese writer, warns us against European homogenisation, which today "is almost ridiculous when it

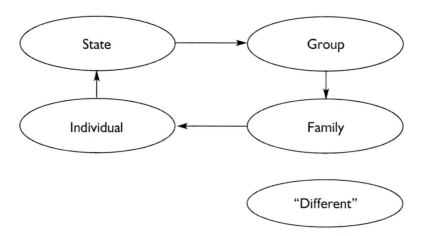

Figure 1.2.   The tendency to become "one".

legislates on the size of chicken cages or the kind of headwear that meat carvers should use. We do not have comedians who are up to the task of satirising this crisis of puberty . . ." (2008)
Perhaps we do not need comedians, but we need thinkers who should take these symptoms seriously (cf. Moguillansky, 2003).

Bullying,[5] a new name for an old phenomenon which has grown to become a major concern affecting more than 40% of the school population, according to the Brazilian Multidisciplinary Centre for the Studies of School Bullying (CEMEOBES.com.br, accessed in 2012), would be one of the initial forms taken by the demand for uniformity and exclusion. It is a product of the clash between society and individual narcissism (all that is equal is good; it is incorporated and accepted; all that is different is bad and should be expelled). Today it is a classmate, next a minority, then a foreign country: the composition of the psychological grounds for genocide or war is not unlike these childhood group phenomena.

Fromm maintains that an authoritarian state requires authoritarian personalities who respect power and who are willing to submit to it. They identify themselves with it by attacking the weak.

Bullying also occurs in the case of the executive who, after years of submitting to an authoritarian boss, has temporary outbursts of aggression against his wife or daughters, displacing in these acts the repressed violence in the asymmetrical relationship he had with his boss (Sluzki, 2006). The effect of moral harassment in business organisations, also called organisational bullying, goes far beyond the walls of the company and produces devastating effects on the families of their employees.

Even though their discourse and intention are both antiauthoritarian and democratic, many institutions in the modern state (from universities to companies) help to produce authoritarian personalities who humiliate and abuse subordinates and women (as much as 63% of the female workforce in Brazil is said to be victims of bullying, especially Afro-Brazilian women) (Heloani & Barreto, 2008).

The intersubjective and the intrasubjective: a clinical case

The following is the case of Vinicius, an obese preadolescent, and a victim of humiliation due to school bullying.

Vinicius reminded me of single or youngest children who have the fantasy that they have ruined the reproductive capacity of their mother: after his birth there would not be any new life, as if the mould had been broken. This fantasy produces the idea in these children, as was the case with Vinicius, that their mother might die at any moment or that she might want to take revenge, killing the child. With regard to their peers, these children develop a pathological "avoidance of rivalry", and might sometimes present inhibitions and phobias.

This aggressive fantasy produced in Vinicius feelings of guilt, and a search for punishment. In the family therapy sessions, he would exhibit the bruises produced by his classmates' aggression and spoke about the periods he spent in the school infirmary as if they were victories. After a few sessions, it was evident that it was very important for Vinicius to victimise himself and to make it clear that he had not ruined anybody, especially not his mother, who complained of having put on weight after his birth, and that he was the one who was hurt. That way, he could control the omnipotent and guilty fantasy of having irretrievably hurt his mother's body and his parents' sex life, preventing the birth of other children.

His mother was overprotective of Vinicius, complaining regularly at the school and arguing with the headteacher (who will require a separate paragraph). She also defended him against his father's criticisms. All this produced in him a sensation of triumph in his Oedipal rivalry, bringing about a consequent increase in his guilt and additional reinforcement of his self-humiliating behaviours.

Playing the clown and asking the other children to beat him, Vinicius restarted the cycle of exhibitionistic victimisation. He was the prisoner of a paradoxical behaviour in which he imagined he won when he lost, reinforced the inhibition of his aggression, and was setting himself up for a destiny as a loser.

Their worry about Vinicius provided his parents with the opportunity for a defensive delay necessary to avoid facing the conflicts between them. Vinicius's father shouted "like mad" and his eyes popped out of his head every time he scolded him for his inability to defend himself when his mates humiliated him and called him "a cow" (Vinicius was fat, but he was also the strongest in his class, he could have easily defeated any of his "rival peers"). His father did not pay attention to the analyst's advice about lowering his voice when he scolded Vinicius, since this would only frighten the boy even more when his mates or anybody else shouted at him. For several sessions, the therapist tried to explain that the father's reaction was exaggerated and it looked as if he was experiencing the aggressive acts against his son as if they were addressed to him.

His father remembered then that when he was a child he used to wet himself when his own father (Vinicius's grandfather) shouted at him at the top of his voice, that he trembled with fear when he had to face any of his classmates. He had also been the strongest in his class. In addition, his own mother was the only one who comforted him, as was now the case with his son.

Vinicius seemed to communicate the message of being an only child or a spoiled child, possibly as a way to make up for his feelings of humiliation in the face of segregation and the attacks he had to bear. This reinforced the circuit of his exclusion from the group. Vinicius challenged his mates to beat him, showing (at one moment in the cycle) an attitude of superiority that was later conflated with the privileges derived from the special attention received from both the nurse and his mother.[6]

It is important to pay attention to the tendency of the group, as it reflects the tendency of society to be one (a tendency to uniformity), expelling the one who is different, and also to pay attention to the intrapsychic aspects, the personal conflicts of the one who is excluded. To this effect, we often see that the attitudes of schools with regard to bullying are divided between those who assess the importance of group phenomena and those who leave them aside and look at the problem as if it were part of the pathology of the victim.

The challenge lies in analysing at the intersection of intrapsychic and family processes with group and social processes in order to be able to act efficiently.

The tendency of the therapist or the school to protect the victims might lead them to overlook the participation of the victims themselves in the phenomenon of bullying. Nevertheless, the comprehension of those unconscious dynamics should not lessen institutional responsibility in the face of group violence.

It merits pointing out that the pedagogical ideology in Vinicius's school was guided by the headteacher, a former martial arts trainer. While not acknowledging it, he encouraged a pedagogy of humiliation, according to which it was necessary to learn how to defend oneself, a new version, regarding group behaviour, of the old adage: Spare the rod, spoil the child. His leadership facilitated, if not encouraged, group humiliation.

Being a victim of numerous humiliations and not confronting them, as was the case with Vinicius, whose rebellions were systematically squashed, might structure the subject into resentment. This resentment, with its torturing fantasies of revenge, manifests in one of two ways: the subject is set up as a privileged victim (cf. Kancyper, 2006), or as an avenger (Figure 1.3).

In the first case (a privileged victim), the subject might pathologically follow a strategy of chronic melancholia, continuing with his role as a privileged victim, filled with a paralysing resentment. Possibly this would have been the case with Vinicius, if he had not undergone treatment.

In the second case (an avenger), the subject might follow a depressive–psychopathic alternation or a depressive justification of psychopathic actions. This has been the case with adolescents who acted as avengers of their own exclusion and entered their schools with guns, killing teachers and students, which has occurred in several countries and has been widely covered in the media.

Eventually, the subject might leave that circuit and organise himself as somebody capable of facing adversity, responding to it with no

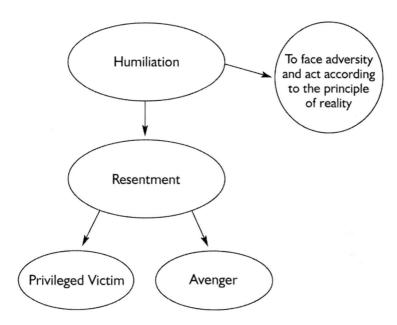

Figure 1.3. Destinies of humiliation.

inhibitions, structuring his aggressiveness in accordance with external reality.

Regarding bullying, we can ask ourselves the question Albert Einstein asks Freud at the end of his letter to him, foreseeing the possibility of war (Freud, 1933b, p. 183), "Is there a possibility to direct the psychic evolution of men so that they become capable of resisting the psychoses of hatred and destruction?" Freud answered that every human action is the product of a mixture of urges from Eros (life) and Thanatos (destruction). When men are incited to war, noble motives (expressed) are aroused in them, as well as subordinate motives (which they keep concealed). "The pleasure of attacking and destroying is probably one which is kept concealed", says Freud (1933b, p. 187). He adds that the existence of that pleasure is also asserted by the innumerable cruelties in history and in everyday life, in which conscious ideal motives are frequently reinforced by unconscious destructive desires.

Freud later states that the demand of religions, "love thy neighbour as thou love thyself", is easier to formulate than to achieve. In spite of the fact that, from time immemorial, humanity has been subjected to a process he calls "civilising" to which we owe "the best of our development and a good part of our ills", for him "the ideal would be a human community that should submit the life of their urges to the dictatorship of reason". He also put forward a "therapy" that acknowledged that war is a product of the destructive urge; so everything that strengthens emotional bonds, the mutual identification among men, the encouragement of intellect and the fear derived from the effects of war should operate as antagonists to this urge (Freud, 1933b).

In all institutional prescriptions to fight school, workplace, or cyber bullying, all these elements must be present, in doses adequate to the institution: a strengthening of affective bonds and positive identifications, an incentive to intellectual development and the fear of the consequences of aggressive conduct, and, certainly, the institutional interdiction of violence (Figure 1.4).

Parameters for considering shame

Nietzsche was one of the few philosophers who took into account the rise of shame and included it as part of a kind of ethics (arguable and dangerous) for which he proposes a historical genealogy. For Nietzsche, the lofty values of the aristocracy dominant in Ancient Greece, "Health, youth, sexuality, pride in one's own strength, the expression of desires for power without ill-feigned modesty, etc."

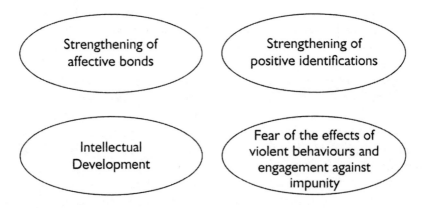

Figure 1.4.   Prevention and intervention in bullying situations.

have been replaced, due to "philosophy", by the values along whose lines we are still being educated: "shame of the body, shame of sexuality, false modesty, love of poverty, self-resignation not to live a full life, death wishes, etc." In his opinion, the latter constitute our "slave morals" and he suggests we should abandon them (Nicola, 2005, pp. 178–180.)

In his first model of the psychotherapy of hysteria, Freud (with Breuer) (1895d) is guided by the elements of conscience in approaching the repressed trauma that would produce the symptom. Among these elements, shame and disgust are infallible compasses. Shame was a sign inside the conscience of a certain element that was repressed in the unconscious but, at the same time, was an affect whose existence in the conscience could cause repression of the element that motivated the shame.

The consideration of shame was very frequent in Freud's works until his first revision of *Three Essays* (1905d), while humiliation, although not developing into a complete metapsychological term, is a part, implicitly or explicitly, of case histories as well as of theoretical texts, especially in items related to narcissism (Puchades, 2005, p. 119).

Initially, Freud thought that shame and disgust arose with the emergence of sexuality in puberty, which gave a retroactive meaning to traumatic impressions that occurred in early periods of the child's life. These traumatic impressions that now generate shame in their new significance, produced by the knowledge of sexuality, were repressed, with the consequent appearance of symptoms. He thought that in a neurotic subject, self-condemnation for having participated, or for having been induced to participate as a child, in a sexual act turns easily into shame *when the other knows about it* (Freud, 1896, p. 157). Much later, Freud connects the emergence of shame and guilt with the presence in the child of forbidden unconscious sexual urges towards the father, agent of the punishment. These unconscious desires would appear in the child's conscience through fantasies in which another child is beaten: the action of beating would be the substitute for a sexual action that, due to the repression, was blurred into an indefinite agent and subject–victim of the punishment.

Kinston reminds us that in the same way as the action corresponding to guilt is the need for punishment, the action corresponding to anguish is escape, and the action produced by shame is the need to hide (Figure 1.5).

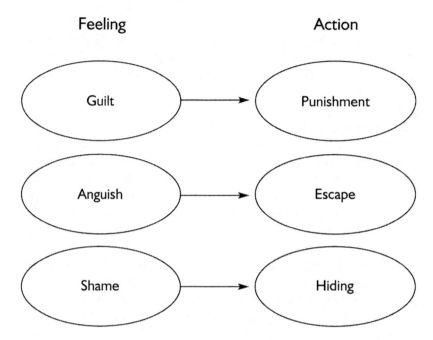

Figure 1.5.   The correlation between feelings and actions.

Freud quotes Homer,

> Away from your homeland and from all that is loved, wandering in
> strange countries, after much suffering, overwhelmed with worries,
> miserable and deserted, you will dream every night that you approach
> your homeland and you will see it shine, painted in beautiful colours.
> Sweet images, delicate and loved ones will come to meet you; then
> you will notice you walk wounded, naked, covered with dust.
> Unspeakable shame and anguish will invade you, you will try to cover
> and conceal yourself, and you will wake up drenched in sweat.
> (Freud, 1900a, p. 246)

As we see, Freud presents from his earliest work the dimension of the
other: shame is a social feeling that includes predominantly the eyes
of the other. It is the other who can see that one feels shame in one's
face, and it is at that moment when it reveals itself through blushing.

Several authors describe shame as part of a continuum; it would
be the intermediate link between mindlessness (the most regressive
moment) and the feeling of guilt (the most mature moment) in a

passage from "invulnerability to vulnerability, from pre-compassion to concern" (Conran, 1993, p. 839) (Figure 1.6). In turn, according to Lewis (1971), shame would correspond to a negative assessment of the self while guilt would correspond to the negative assessment of an action.

Kinston (1983) points out that the absence of the term "shame" in Laplanche and Pontalis's dictionary (1973) indicates the scarce attention paid by psychoanalysis to this emotion in the past. It has been called the "Cinderella of unpleasant emotions" (Rycroft, 1968) for good reason. Kinston attempts to summarise how the term was dealt with in psychoanalytic literature/

1. Shame is situated within the social bond as an expression of sexual urge or defence (Freud).
2. Shame is not taken into account or is mentioned in passing (Laplanche and Pontalis; Winnicott, Kernberg, Segal).
3. Shame is indistinguishable from guilt (Hartman, Sandler, and Jacobson).
4. Shame, for Fenichel, is a defence against exhibitionism, and can be qualified as signal shame, operating like a function, which anticipates the emergence of situations where there could be a paralysing invasion of the ego by this affection. Or it can be an

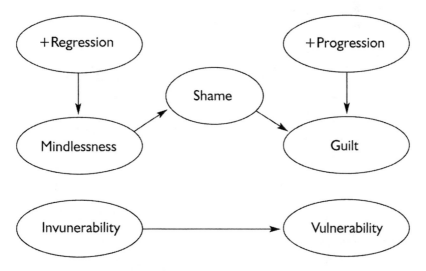

Figure 1.6. Shame, regression, and progression.

automatic shame, where this invasion could not be avoided. Kohut thinks that the invasion of the ego by an original exhibitionism of the grandiose child-*self* would bring about "painful shame".

5.   Shame is associated with identity, narcissism (Erikson, Lichtenstein).

Kinston puts forward an interesting description of *self narcissism* that would express the evolution of the child towards autonomy, and a *narcissism of the object*, in which the child would be subjected to the wishes of narcissistic parents who would punish with lack of affection any transgression of their wishes and who would consider any differentiation as cruelty against them (the parents). The attempt to be different from that symbiotic demand would cause shame to emerge from an ego that was still immature when seeking a relationship with others. Submitting to his parents' wishes (narcissism of the object), the subject would stop feeling shame; he would become shame-less. "The price of individuation is shame", states Kinston (1983, p. 26). (cf. Figure 1.7).

Shame would first emerge as a sign of a process of differentiation in the face of parental demands and models and, later, as a result of the attempt to move away from those models and demands, already

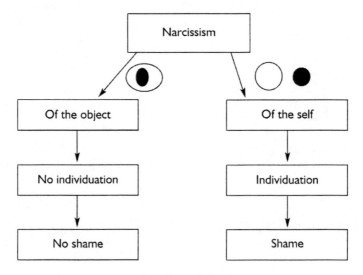

Figure 1.7.   Narcissism of the object and of the self.

incorporated into the ideal of the ego.[7] And in the course of treatment, its presence may be used as an indicator of the progress towards individuation. Velasco (2002, p. 90) says, "the dialogue we can establish in moments of shame permits the loosening of unconscious convictions . . . (and the progress) towards individuation" (translated for this edition).

The expression of a forbidden affection, the assumption of a banned identity trait, the invasion of conscience by a fantasy (sexual, incestuous, aggressive, exhibitionistic) restrained by the ego ideal leads to a desire for a regressive escape towards that ideal to recover the protection of undifferentiation which was lost in the attempt to get away from parents' wishes or from the ideal. That regressive move is frequently preceded by a sensation expressed in a wish to be swallowed up by (Mother) Earth and on other occasions is manifested by uncontrolled corporeal sensations (blushing, trembling, etc.).

It is as if shame were announcing an attempt to be differentiated on the one hand, and on the other hand, a regressive move away from symbolisation in the direction of the unified body (between the child and his parents) of narcissism (cf. Figure 1.8).

"Shame signals the confession of a defeat, the disclosure of a weakness, the loss of appearances and of dignity, that can reach the point of imagining his internal world exposed to the eyes of the other", says Green (2004, p. 58, translated for this edition). He describes those eyes, pursuing and external, as if they were denouncing an indignity that

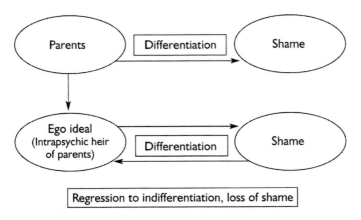

Figure 1.8.   Differentations of shame.

calls for a desperate search for space away from those eyes. He marks the difference with the self-observation of melancholia, which would keep its internal nature. This assertion is complemented with the now classic comment of Lacan, cited by Green: "A gaze is the lost object which is unexpectedly recovered in the explosion of shame, through the appearance of the other" (translated for this edition).

Clinical vignettes

1: Juan

Juan, a fifty-five-year-old businessman, wants to distance his son Carlos from his prosperous businesses. Carlos works for his father only a few hours a month, but nevertheless supports his own family with the generous compensation provided by his father, besides having always accepted innumerable presents, trips abroad, his own sumptuous house, and the like.

Juan left Carlos's mother over twenty years ago, a separation she never accepted. Despite all the support he receives from his father, Carlos has decided not to invite him to his birthday party, arguing that his mother would not be at ease and that, if his father is willing, they can go for a meal together any time to celebrate his birthday on their own.

This motivates a session, requested by Juan. During the treatment of the parent–son bond, it is clear that Carlos is wholly identified with his mother's wishes. Carlos's wife has been enlisted in the family dynamic and acts as an extension of her mother-in-law. In addition, she looks upon the relationship of her father-in-law with his new young fiancée as a potential threat, representing a dangerous example of a way out in any future marriage crisis with Carlos.

Carlos is not at all ashamed when he excludes his father, to whom he owes so much. The fact that he is undifferentiated from his mother's wishes protects him from feeling shame (and/or guilt). His father reproaches him and calls him "shameless", with psychological propriety (cf. Kinston, 1983).

2: Pedro

Twenty-eight-year-old Pedro, after two years of a passionate affair with a seductive and elusive married woman who shares his passion only in part, notices that his beloved is moving away from him. She is afraid the situation will be made public (as a result of a careless exposure) and she also fears that Pedro will somehow reveal his consuming passion. To protect herself from this risk, she tells her husband that Pedro, a colleague she had introduced to the family as a new friend, is harassing her. Pedro, suddenly, feels shame and humiliation.

In the sessions, Pedro relates that his love affair started when his first child was born and he felt his wife was deserting him to look after the baby. This situation took him back to the birth of his own brother, five years younger than him, and to the family stories about his own feelings of exclusion many years ago.

The passion he felt for his lover helped him to conceal the feelings of rejection that rose up again after the birth of his child. He adds that while the affair lasted, he was careless and did not avoid the public eye. In that period, there was no emergence of the feelings of shame and humiliation that appear when his beloved—fearing the affair would ruin her marriage—decided to put an end to it. From then on, Pedro isolates himself in response to a sensation of shame and at the same time the feeling of humiliation makes him resentful and vengeful: he threatens to disclose the secrets his lover has shared with him in intimacy as well as to make public that she has been unfaithful to her husband.

He tries to justify his vengeful ideas on the grounds that he was terribly hurt and he felt betrayed when she decided to go back to her husband and make this decision public, because he imagines their small social network knew about their relationship and now they know she is back with her husband.

Humiliation due to desertion comes together with a feeling of shame, where the dominant component is the public element, the gaze of society and the family, from which there is no escape.

"Of the three components of the superego, self-observation, moral conscience and the function of the ideal, Freud assigns the greatest importance to the first" (Green, 2004, p. 66, translated for this edition) (Figure 1.9).

The function of the external gaze, omnipresent in shame, forces the ashamed person into "permanent flight". The observing instance contained in the superego–ideal ego system is projected on the external world, giving the sensation of being watched by all.

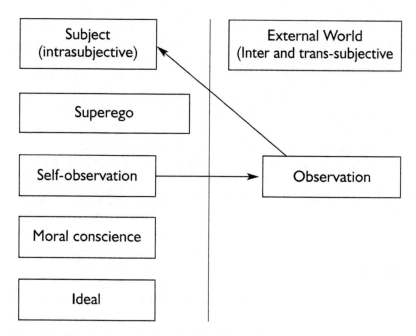

Figure 1.9. The components of the superego.

As a defensive response, sometimes the subject assumes the role of revealer of the shameful acts of the other. It is like a transformation in reverse, an identification with the shame that pursues him, thus becoming a relentless pursuer of the one who put him to shame before all others, who could have seen his shame, his weakness.[8]

We see, then, that initially, passion, in its dimension of narcissistic regression, lets Pedro feel free of shame (shame-less). The rupture of the narcissistic structure favours the emergence of shame and, with it, the need to give his feelings an outlet. Through projection, he starts a crusade of accusations to put to shame the person who has shamed him. He does so by telling several people certain details that, according to his morals, he would not have mentioned if he had not taken offence (Figure 1.10)

3: José

José, aged fifty-eight, is a politician in an inland town, married to Maria, thirty-one, who left her job as his secretary when she became his second wife.

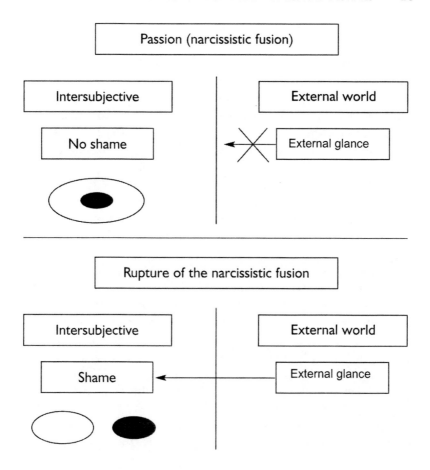

Figure 1.10.   How the rupture of the narcissistic fusion facilitates the emergence of shame.

In a session with both partners, after an absence of a few months, Maria speaks about the continual slights she receives from José's son and daughter-in-law and recounts her misfortunes and her humiliation, especially when they call her an incompetent hostess. "It is the last straw; she is having lunch in my house and snubs my housekeeping."

In one session, José is aloof, silent, as if he were angry. As this has already happened in other sessions during the intermittent treatment, the analyst thinks José feels he is being cornered. Maria says the previous year was difficult because she had been diagnosed with a hormonal condition and prescribed drugs that had stopped her menstrual periods, besides having undergone surgery. "When I stopped taking the medicines I felt well and the periods went back to normal, but he pressed me to consult a fertility specialist, since we were going to get married. I was not in any hurry ..." He interrupts, "It so happens that I am a responsible person; I wanted to make sure we could have children, be able to have them." The specialist concluded that José had no fertility problems but that her case was more complicated. "I knew it," she says.

They discuss several situations related to his children again. She claims he punishes her with long periods of silence and says that he is very demanding and nothing she does is good enough.

The analyst comments that the relationship with his former family is going along quite well, better than before, and she is quite competent in managing such a complicated household. He adds that she seems to feel he disrespects her with his urgency to have children. Also, that he makes her feel she is no good in her reproductive role even though she considers that had not been the agreement between them. Perhaps, the analyst continues, she feels undervalued and fears that if she cannot be a good hostess for his children (that is, get pregnant), it will be impossible for him to accept her. All these worries prevent her from noticing his insecurities, which lie elsewhere, and are not really related to infertility.

The therapist then addresses José and tells him that his haste in consulting a specialist about the couple's capacity to conceive has to do not only with his responsibility (as had been said before) but also with another problem: his male potency, a frequent concern with middle-aged men. Perhaps his fear substitutes reproduction for potency.

José says that the reason why he did not speak for a week was not that he was angry, but that he was ashamed because he had not been able to have sexual relations. Now, listening to the therapist, he feels he had been engaged in navel-gazing the whole previous year and had not paid attention to her, her hormonal ailment, her surgery. The therapist asserts that worrying about male potency brings about a kind of blindness.

In this situation of dual shame, she feels she is not in line with her own ideal, which demands motherhood in marriage. Because of this, sadly, she does not pay attention to her own real physical suffering and submits to her husband's overriding wishes to consult doctors for a purpose which is not important to her at the moment. This is reinforced by his behaviour: he is overwhelmed by his own shame, and he tries to escape through a paranoid elaboration centred in an attitude of having taken offence and a regressive withdrawal before her suffering look, which he interprets as accusatory due to his impotence. The situation made José feel ashamed, and he defensively turned it into humiliation and paranoid withdrawal.

When we approach the symptom of shame in the intersubjective space, we can reverse misunderstandings in which the other regressively becomes a representative or an executor of the ideal, modifying it, magnifying or diminishing it, or even giving it a different meaning. Shame emerges, even in the framework of a love relationship, with the reappearance of fantasies that weaken the subjects in relation to the ideal (Figure 1.11).

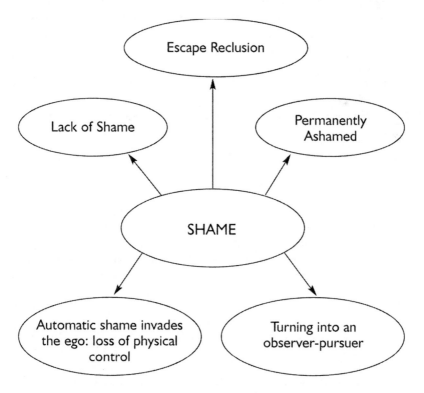

Figure 1.11. The emergence of shame and its effects.

In this chapter, I have shown some of the dynamics and outcomes of shame and humiliation. I reviewed several hypotheses that link these emotions to social and cultural situations as well as to different evolutionary stages. I have also given examples of the way they work within the complexity of clinical systems, which is enriched with a proper acquaintance with these concepts.

There are other possible mechanisms and outcomes for these feelings, some of which were mentioned briefly, and others which were not described.

The relationship between shame and depression, paranoia, guilt in general, and survivor's guilt will be examined on another occasion.[8]

Notes

1. Early on, Freud thought that the origin of neuroses could be related to a trauma which he later described as sexual, caused by child abuse exercised by an adult in the child's social environment. As he advanced in his theory, Freud abandoned the seduction theory, replacing it by the dominant influence of intrapsychic fantasy on the production of neuroses. This led him to develop the importance of the Oedipus complex, but removed him from external causality, later taken up by Ferenczi.

2. Aulagnier thought that for the future identity of a child, a mother's reverie during pregnancy was of the utmost importance, when in her mind she would build up his representation, and not only during that period, but throughout his life the ego was nourished by external reality. She was

> moving away from the solipsism that reduces the construction of a subject to his own representations where historical truth is mere fantasy projected on the past, and conceptualises a historian-ego, dependent on his historisation of the identifying process and on external reality. (Bigliani, 2009, p. 164, translated for this edition).

This ego

> would then be constituted by a set of identifications, a product of enunciations that were produced about the subject by significant others, and the regard of these others who propose to the child's ego representations which will consolidate an identifying construction. (Bigliani, 2009, p. 164, translated for this edition)

3. The emancipation of the Jews occurred over the period of the eighteenth to the nineteenth century in Europe, a time when the expansion of the ideas of equality and their political corollary, a progressive extension of citizenship, were providing Jews with civil rights that eventually made them similar to Gentiles (earlier in France, after the French Revolution, later in Austria).

4. It is worth remembering that genocides do not belong exclusively to modern states; they have been a constant throughout history. We have only to look at the times of the Crusades down to the more recent examples of extermination of the original inhabitants in the Americas from Canada to Argentina where the original people were systematically wiped out by the colonising countries. Neither should we forget the slave trade in the Americas, during which ten million Africans are estimated to have died just in crossing the ocean. According to Littell (2007), the modern state has changed from one method of extermination, conquest and slavery, to another—its industrial structure.

5. Dan Olwens coined the term *bullying* in Bergen, Norway, more than forty years ago based on a study of a case of three adolescents who committed suicide after they had been abused by their peers. As a result of his studies, Olwens (me) developed school programs for the reduction of bullying in schools, which were successful in Norway and were later used in other countries in Europe and North America.

6. Freud thought that the intolerance of the masses was particularly directed towards those peoples who assumed the attitude of privileged children (Freud, 1939a).

7. During adolescence, mourning processes such as those classically described by Aberastury and Knobel (1984) for the child's body image, the child's identity, the parents or the family of childhood, and the fantasies of bisexuality are processed. The subject is gripped by a great deal of insecurity during the construction of this "new adolescent ego". This implies a permanent "autoscopy" while making an effort to differentiate themselves from the parents of their childhood and from their wishes. This differentiation makes living a shameful period, undermining the youth in relation to actions of impairment or teasing from others. As a defence they frequently become permanent "shamers" of others (usually adults). This perhaps led Nasio to say that ". . . teenagers suffer from a growth neurosis nurtured by a childish and exaggerated fear of being humiliated" (2012, p. 50, translated for this edition).

8. Basak (2009) tells us of the revision Osamu Kitayama made in 1985 (Kitayama & Matuki, 2004) to Japanese myths, where such prohibition is

manifested in the context of stories where we can identify passive and active shame. In all of the stories, wives produced something (food, children, jewels), but the husband was not allowed to see the production process, which included characteristics of form, exhibitions, or postures shameful to women. When this prohibition was broken, the wife ran away in what was described as passive shame. In another myth, Izanami, when her husband saw her with her body covered by worms while she produced deities and Japanese islands, she felt overwhelmed with "passionate rage" and "hurtful shame", an example of active shame. Benedict (1946) described what she called a "culture of shame" in Japan and specified this affection as one of the principal organisers of human relationships.

9. Primo Levi (1965, 1989) describes the "shame of staying alive" in prisoners and survivors of German concentration camps during the Second World War and he even recounts the shame of the prisoners when the Russian soldiers arrived at the camp where he was a prisoner at the end of the war.

CHAPTER TWO

Comment I

Rodolfo Moguillansky

.

I n order to present my commentary, I will divide the subjects tackled by Bigliani into different sections, detailed under the subheadings below.

Significances arising from the internal world and those instituted by interactions that include us

Psychoanalysis usually proposes an opposition between the psychoanalytic paradigm, focused on the study of significances arising from the internal world, and the systemic paradigm, which considers this world a black box and so focuses on the significances arising from the interactive network in which we are included.

My suggestion is that, although we cannot deny we emphasise different points, I do not believe our differences are immeasurable.

Our challenge is to be able to minimise the gap between our views and positions through our exchanges.

Immeasurability is mentioned in the philosophy of science (Feyerabend, 1970, 1999), in reference to the impossibility of comparing two theories because they do not share a common theoretical language.

Two theories are immeasurable when there is no way to compare them because in order to bridge the gaps, we have to try to bring together our objects of observation, our languages of observation.[1]

Reading Bigliani's introduction confirms my impression that we can have a discussion together with Sluzki—not only due to the deep affection we feel for him. At the same time, we can assess our respective positions while observing and theorising on the effects of this interaction. I mention this because, as I read it, I share with Bigliani—perhaps because our psychoanalytic practice has made us deal with individuals, couples, families, and institutions—the fact that we do not believe in the paradigm prevailing in the psychoanalytic world of the 1930s, which considered that any threat that undermined the (theoretical) importance of psychic reality was threatening the force and reliability of the psychoanalytic movement.

We belong to a generation that attended the lectures of Enrique Pichon Rivière at the Buenos Aires School of Social Psychology and was trained at the Lanus Hospital, where we learned clinical psychiatry at the same time as we studied Freud and the classics of psychoanalysis, and we were deeply moved by Bateson, Jackson, Haley, and Weakland's essay (1956) in which they established the theory of the double bond, while also reading the early compilation about family therapy by Boszormenyi-Nagy and Framo (1965). We also attended, together with Carlos Sluzki, the first Congress on Family Therapy in Argentina in 1970, at the School of Medicine, Buenos Aires University,[2] while we reflected on the subject of power when reading *The Power Tactics of Jesus Christ*, by Haley (1969), which, together with other texts, launched us into the study of the systems of relationships patients were immersed in and of the mechanisms by which the system itself was ill and would make them ill. (In fact, Sluzki preceded us in that route, as he was a faculty member at Bigliani's and my psychiatric residency programme, and also the factotum and president of the above-mentioned pioneering international Congress.)

I dare say that our vision as psychoanalysts has led us to appropriate the rich heritage of psychoanalysis and, at the same time, to be open to ideas involving a change of direction in the production of meaning, different from the direction classically indicated by psychoanalysis. This change of direction never assumed the early psychoanalytic paradigm as its own. Any reference to the influence of the social environment was considered resistential.[3]

We are also part of a line of thought that included the foundational effect of culture and the idea that not only are we the result of what impulse determines, but we are also defined by the social network in which we live. It must be said that there has been a delay in making this line of thought a part of the "mainstream" of psychoanalysis.

Psychoanalytic contributions that account for the instituting role of the other

I agree with Bigliani when he mentions the ground covered by the contributions of psychoanalysis to the introduction of the new perspective in authors such as Lacan (1964–1965) with the Freudian recovery of the construction of a subject in whom the presence of the other was fundamental; Bion, with his formulations on groups (1958) or his introduction of the capacity of maternal reverie as being fundamental to symbolic production (Bion, 1962); Aulagnier (1975) when she defined the human condition based on the situation of the anticipatory meeting between a mother and her unborn child; Kaës (1989; Kaës, Faimberg, Enriquez, & Baranes, 1993) with his emphasis on considering *transindividual formations* as shapes of psychic reality forming part of the hard core of the unconscious; Rousillon (1985), when he incorporated the concept of paradox—studied by the Palo Alto researchers—to understand narcissistic pathologies, etc.

Psychoanalytic contributions that make the symptom intelligible in the family context

I also agree on the topic of the role played by several psychoanalytic authors who made an effort to render the symptom intelligible in the family context. This is part of a long tradition, starting with the pioneering works of Dicks (1970)[4]; Willi (1976, 2004)[5]; Laing (1961, 1967, Laing & Esterson, 1967, Laing, Phillipson, & Lee, 1966); Ackerman (1958); Ferreira (1966); Sluzki (1993, 2004); Ruffiot et al. (1981); Berenstein (1976, 1981); Puget and Berenstein (1988); Eiguer (1983); Losso (2001); Merea (2005); Spivacow (2005), and many others (including the author of the chapter I am discussing here, Bigliani (2003)).

The interactional and the transgenerational

Returning to my comment, Bigliani´s narrative about Freud's family story, which he uses as clinical material, is altogether thrilling. In order to make it comprehensible, he combines his own ideas with those proposed by Puget and Kaës, essential for understanding how social insertion is imposed on the subject and includes him in a history that precedes and succeeds him.

He asserts—along with Puget—that imposed history has an unconscious quality and turns the subject into a transmitter and an actor of a social organisation in which he plays active and passive roles at the same time. He echoes Kaës when he points out that the question of the subject is increasingly defined in the intersubjective space, more precisely in the space and time of the generation of the family and group.

Psychoanalysts consider the question of precedence of the other, or of more than one other, in the destiny of an individual as a challenge to the understanding of psychic life, where the ego can come into being or finds difficulties in creating itself.

I would add to Bigliani´s words on the matter the contributions of Abraham and Torok (1978): that which we transmit is precisely that which we cannot hold, we cannot retain, we cannot remember: lack, illnesses, shame, what we have repressed, lost objects still mourned. Torok and Abraham considered that shameful situations, or those involving non-elaborated mourning, in the Freudian sense, that have not been incorporated through introjections (a concept they use to account for what is internalised through play, fantasy, projection, and a variety of unconscious mechanisms) will give way to psychic suffering and become a trauma. It is from this traumatic situation that "alienating identifications", as later authors called them, are derived.

They use the term "alienating significances" to refer to the transmission through identifications of that which suffers from lack of significance.

Uniformity, violence against that which is different. Narcissism in slight differences, one of the origins of humiliation

In this attempt to build bridges, I deem Bigliani´s reflections on "bullying"[6] a real find, especially when, in addition to accounting for the problem created by its practice among children and adolescents, he relates it to the demand for uniformity and exclusion, produced by the clash between society and individual narcissism. He asserts that the modern state presents a demand for uniformity in its task of creating a reality and in its attempt to dominate and control the population.

Uniformity and the Utopia of a world without conflicts

I found it very helpful, when thinking of Bigliani´s statements about uniformity, to read Gray's reflections.[7] Gray, a professor at the London School of Economics, has been contributing to publications since 1987 about the yearning of society and man for a world in harmony, with no conflicts. He states that Utopian ideologies, which shaped a large portion of the history of the last century, favoured this yearning. Even though these ideologies claimed to be based on science and rejected traditional creeds, believing they were on the side of human enlightenment, they have played a harmful role in the history of humanity. Gray thinks that these systems of belief, which advocate the elimination of evil in the world, are, in fact, terribly dangerous to humanity because they have almost always generated movements that include violence and end up degenerating into totalitarianism.

Humiliation and the elimination of the "different" ones

I also agree with Bigliani when he asserts that the clinical observation of humiliation is closely connected to the effect produced by beliefs which are intent on discrediting the other because he is different, on attacking him, on despising him, on killing him.

Humiliation, "otherness", and "being with another one"

The theme of uniformity mentioned by Bigliani in his chapter has interested me for a number of years (Moguillansky, 2003, 2004). I would like to propose in addition that to broach this topic of uniformity, it is important to make the distinction between bonds in which we participate and those that involve us as subjects, between "otherness"[8] and "being with another one".[9]

My suggestion is that all "wholes", when they are instituted, unify those who *compose* them, and, at the same time, expel that which does not share the feeling of the community, which I would call *Otherness*. This Otherness is that which is rejected, condemned by the "whole", that which *should not be*, or even *what the "whole" states it is not*, the other, we should actually say the Otherness, which is not part of the *whole*. A consequence of this definition is that subjects who are part of the Otherness are usually ill-treated by those included in the whole, as if they were outside this world, who may be, who should be, humiliated and destroyed.

To flesh out the definition of Otherness, I will attempt to provide an ostensible image of how I describe that feeling. With that in mind, I quote a paragraph from the novel *The Desire*, by Hugo Claus (1978), in which the Belgian writer describes harshly what happens at "The Unicorn", the pub in the village where the novel is set:

> Anyway, at the Unicorn we used to get on well with everybody. Sometimes we have a row with someone and there are a few we would beat up in the dark if we could, but even with those we get on well. They would have to be real shit to turn them away from our tables. I refer to the regulars, of course. The one who enters unexpectedly, if we don't know him, can count on our total and complete contempt. The one who doesn't gamble does not exist. (p. 143)

I think it is helpful, then, as a contribution to Bigliani's statement, to make a distinction between Otherness—the non-regulars at the Unicorn in Claus's *Desire*, people with whom you do not speak or who are stigmatised in the dialogue—and what I call "being with another one". I say *I am with and talk with another one* when I consider that other to be another subject, he has an existence like me, and in that existence I acknowledge his total diversity from me.

The problem of the intersubjective and the intrasubjective: Vinicius

In order to discuss the problem of the intersubjective and the intrasubjective, Bigliani tells us the story of an obese preadolescent, a victim of humiliation due to school bullying.

Proposed theoretical outline of the intrapsychic

Bigliani establishes some of his theoretical points from the very beginning. Drawing on Melanie Klein, he states that he shares her idea that some youngest or only children often fantasise that they have ruined the reproductive capacity of their mother. He goes on to say that because of this, they believe there will not be any life after them, as if the mould were broken. Owing to this fantasy, they fear their mother might die suddenly or that she might want to take revenge and kill the child, which accounts for these children developing inhibitions and phobias.

Bigliani assumes that, owing to this fantasy of aggression, Vinicius was overcome by a feeling of guilt and, as a consequence, he sought punishment. Fully convinced of this, Bigliani says that as treatment advanced, the self-victimisation of Vinicius is the way in which his internal world settles the score and makes it clear that he has not ruined anybody, his mother in particular. Bigliani goes on to state, in accordance with the initial outline informing his data, that this was how Vinicius was able to control his omnipotent fantasy of being to blame for having irreparably damaged his mother's body and his parent's life, preventing the birth of siblings.

Considerations of how family interaction and the intrapsychic come together

The mother supports the role of the victim

The scene proposed by Bigliani is rounded out by the description of Vinicius's mother, supporting his role as a "victim", complaining regularly at school and arguing with the headteacher of the school, as well as defending Vinicius from his father's criticisms.

It is important to understand how this author sees Vinicius's victimisation. In this vision, there is a blending of the intrapsychic (the fantasy of having damaged his mother's body) with the interactional (his mother, supporting Vinicius's role as a "victim", complaining at school, arguing with the headteacher, and defending Vinicius from his father).

Interaction strengthens the sensation of triumph in the Oedipal rivalry

The way the pieces of information are organised leads to the conclusion that this scenario produced a sensation of triumph in his Oedipal rivalry, which carried a consequent increase of guilt with renewed reinforcement of his self-humiliating behaviour.

The importance of being a prisoner of a paradoxical behaviour

These considerations would seem to follow Wiener's roadmap—in the sense of a feedback loop—because Vinicius restarted the cycle of exhibitionistic victimisation, playing the clown and asking the other children to beat him. Bigliani uses a theoretical tool created by Bateson and his team and says that Vinicius was a prisoner of a *paradoxical* behaviour, in which he imagined he won when he lost, thus reinforcing the inhibition of his aggressiveness, preparing for his destiny as a loser.

The family makes use of Vinicius's role as a designated patient

He then goes on to consider the role of Vinicius within the family order. According to him, Vinicius's parents took advantage of their worries over him to defensively postpone the conflict between themselves. The ideas present in this description—expressed both by psychoanalysts and systemic authors—lead us to understand the behaviour of a patient as a result of the way his family functions. These contributions have conceptualised notions that are currently part of our language: "designated patient", "scapegoat", "family emergent", etc., which account for the role of family interaction in the appearance of a symptomatic patient.

The circuit described by Bigliani

The circuit described by the author at this point of his clinical report is very interesting.

1. Vinicius's father "went mad" because Vinicius did not defend himself and let the others humiliate him.
2. The analyst intervened to say that his father's yelling frightened the boy and drove him to be frightened when his mates or anybody else shouted at him.
3. The analyst showed that the father's reaction was exaggerated and he seemed to experience the aggressions against his son as if they were addressed to him.

4.   The father's association when he recounts that he wet himself when his own father (Vinicius's grandfather) shouted at him and that he was scared stiff when he had to face any of his schoolmates.

5.   The father's association when he recounts that he had also been the strongest in his class, he had not defended himself, and his own mother was the only one to comfort him, as was now the case with his son.

6.   Bigliani thinks Vinicius felt he was a special, or privileged, child because of the "overprotection granted by his mother" as a way to make up for his feelings of humiliation owing to the attacks and the segregation he was subjected to.

7.   All this, according to the author, reinforces the circuit of exclusion from the group. Vinicius challenged his mates to beat him, exhibiting (at a certain moment in the cycle) an attitude of superiority, later enhanced by the privileges derived from the special care received from his mother and the school nurse.

Interaction

1.   Based on Freud (1939a), Bigliani states that the intolerance of the masses was particularly directed against the people who assumed the role of privileged children.

2.   He states that there is a tendency of the group—mirroring the tendency of society—to be *one*, expelling the one who is different.

Bigliani´s challenge: to make an analysis at the intersection of intrapsychic and family processes with group and social processes in order to intervene effectively

He warns us against the tendency of the therapist or the school to protect the victims, which might lead us to overlook the participation of the victims themselves in the phenomenon. But he also warns us that the comprehension of those unconscious dynamics should not lessen institutional responsibility with regard to violence.

   He makes note of the fact that the pedagogical ideology in Vinicius's school was emphasised by the headteacher, a former martial arts trainer, who encouraged, without acknowledging it, a pedagogy of humiliation.

*Intrapsychic outcomes of humiliation: the role of
privileged victim or avenger*

Bigliani proposes that multiple humiliations, with their rebellions systematically repressed, might cause resentment in the subject. When accompanied by torturing fantasies of revenge, this resentment could choose one of two paths: the subject structures himself as a privileged victim, or as an avenger.

So, he explores the path to becoming a privileged victim: in this case, the subject might establish himself pathologically with a strategy of chronic melancholisation, continuing with his role as the privileged victim, filled with a paralysing resentment. He suggests this might have been the case with Vinicius, if he had not undergone treatment.

In the second case, the role of an avenger, he might establish himself with a depressive–psychopathic alternation or a depressive justification for psychopathic actions.

The confluence of the two outcomes

I discuss this subject in my text (p. 151). I show that Felice, in my narrative, when confronted by humiliation, does not choose between these two different paths. As he causes his revenge to coincide with the simultaneous choice of assuming the role of victim, he commits suicide.

A proposal

Bigliani suggests that we must keep in sight both the intrapsychic and the interactional aspects. Pursuing this thought, he points out that the subject might leave the circuit and organise himself as somebody capable of facing up to adversity, of responding to it without inhibitions, structuring his aggressiveness in accordance with external reality. Stressing the intrapsychic source, he also draws our attention to aggressiveness, basing himself on Freud, and to a certain *naïveté*— as Rousseau does—of a man who is naturally good. He says that to grasp human nature we must remember that the most sublime coexists with the "pleasure of attacking and destroying". However, he does not exhaust the problem raised by bullying by referring only to "nature", since he says that along with this "human nature" all the elements must be present in adequate doses on the role of the institution: a strengthening of affective bonds and positive identifications, the promotion of intellectual development and fear of the consequences of aggressive conduct. He also includes the need for an institutional prohibition of violence.

Parameters proposed by Bigliani when considering shame

In the last part of Bigliani's essay, I find it very interesting to follow his exploration into the consideration of shame in psychoanalytic theory. He points out that it was much more frequent in Freud's works until his first revision of *Three Essays* (1905d). We learn that humiliation, although it does not constitute a metapsychologically complete term, is a part, implicitly or explicitly, of case histories and theoretical texts, especially in questions related to narcissism.

This remark is appealing. It reminded me of Kaës's comment (1989) referring to "the bleeding pact between Freud and Fliess" to stress that in his analysis of "Irma's dream", Freud attaches no importance to Fliess's "malpractice" and focuses his analysis on "Irma's (Emma Eckstein's) fantasies".

An interval with Freud, the role of fantasies, and the role of the other

In this section, I would like to briefly review some of the highlights of Freud's works in order to understand how the notion of shame was created in psychoanalytic theory and the *a posteriori* consequences.

I would point out as the first landmark, in Freud's first complete analysis, that of Elizabeth von R. (Freud, 1895d), he realised that her pains "were part of the conversation", reacting with pain when memories arose. Freud perceived that the symptoms, aside from expressing repressed unconscious ideas and feelings, were also trying to communicate something to another person.

In the course of treatments carried out by Freud in the 1890s, his patients conjured up experiences of sexual seduction that ranged from verbal insinuations to terrifying sexual assaults.

This insistence led him to conclude that the cause of hysteria had to be sought in the action of a childhood sexual trauma. He felt that the appearance of a repressed memory of a disturbing sexual action—

years later—is only possible with patients in whom that experience can activate the mnemic trace of a childhood trauma.

It is at this point that the "scene of seduction" is formed as a theory in Freud's mind. For him in those years, it was the necessary condition for repression, motivated by disgust, shame, or any other negative emotion. So, a few weeks after the dream about Irma's injection, he says, "I am on the trail of the next pre-condition for hysteria, that is, that a primary sexual experience (prior to puberty) accompanied by repulsion and fear must have taken place" (1895d, p. 154).

Freud went on to think, in that period, that conflicts are not mere frustrations or disappointments, they are moral conflicts,[11] and these moral conflicts are marked by unconscious desires, incestuous sexual desires.[12]

Later, Freud completed his theory, "Hysteria is not disavowed sexuality, it is rather disavowed perversion", perversion on the part of the seducer; the patient does not disavow anything, she longs for the agent of seduction instead. Nevertheless, in 1897, as he enquired in detail into these seductions and demonstrated that the "beastlike nature" of the symptoms derived from the seducers' perversions, he did research into a new source of the content of symptoms, that is, fantasies. Fantasies reverted back to something that children had heard by chance at an early age, and understood only later.

In this theoretical context, Freud writes to Fliess a letter (69) dated 21 September 1897 (Freud, 1950, pp. 259–260). In it, he tells Fliess about his disappointment at not finding material truths in his patients' stories: "I have stopped believing in my neurotic patient". Freud thinks he has discovered psychic reality, putting aside historical or social determinants to understand neuroses.

Kaës (1989) states that when Freud "stopped believing in his neurotic patient" he brought to a close the question of binding determinants. At the core of "Freud's self-analysis" or of the "analysis he was doing with Fliess", Kaës says that "as Fliess will not acknowledge his surgical blunder in Emma Eckstein's nasal operation, Freud finds himself in the situation of having to endorse his wilful ignorance if he wants to keep him as a friend" (p. 139, translated for this edition). Kaës goes on to say that Freud

in order to keep the bond with Fliess, must destroy his knowledge of the intrapsychic bonds necessary to return to primitive scenes, and at the same time to serve as a protective construct in the face of authentic memories. (p. 139, translated for this edition)

According to Kaës, Freud absolves Fliess from all responsibility in the case and, at the same time, he attempts to get rid of the idea that he is covering up for Fliess in the dream of Irma's injection.

Kaës's reasoning emboldens him to affirm that Freud's interest in the dream about Irma is to deny his homosexual bond with Fliess. Kaës becomes even bolder when he says that for Freud,

> instituting psychoanalysis is to place in the nucleus of the debate the proton pseudos and the question of the truth of the subject in his/her relationship with that which represents him/her: to Freud, it is Fliess, no less so than Emma. Such a pact remains in the register of neurotic repression: that which has been repressed returns in the initial dream named Irma's injection. The unbearable representation is: if he attributes the cause for everything to Emma's hysteria, it is not so much to give her all the responsibility as to save what should be repressed in his bond with Fliess. (p. 139, translated for this edition)

It is in the context of his relationship (analysis) with Fliess that Freud, according to Kaës, puts aside any hypotheses on bonds when he conceals Fliess's surgical blunder, preserving his homosexual relationship with him. Freud, then, abandoned bonding determinants to deny the homosexual bond, to which Kaës gives the name of "bleeding alliance between Freud and Fliess".

It is from this background that Freud abandons the theory of the "scene of seduction", and affirms—in the famous letter to Fliess of 21 September 1897—his disappointment at not finding material truths in his patients' stories. He understands, then, that a story does not give an account of what actually happened, it only reveals how it was subjectively lived; what has been told, to his way of thinking, has been set in motion by childhood curiosity and is supported by *a prioris* that Freud called "original fantasies". When he abandons the scene of seduction as the cause of hysteria, he does away with the comprehension firmly based on that which had been caused by another subject. He now concentrates on the role of fantasy.

I believe this was also present in the discussion between Freud and Adler, which can be described as an ontological controversy: whether a being is derived from infantile sexuality or is an originally social being.

I believe—as I also stated in my comment to Sluzki's text—that considering it as a contradiction actually weakened psychoanalysis, even though I understand that this kind of elaboration was necessary at the dawn of our discipline. It has been historically typical to feel the need for the sometimes dogmatic assertion of what is new in a new idea, to protect it from possible deviations. This issue extended to the discussion with culturalists and later to the attempts at Freudian– Marxist theorising in the 1960s. It was hard to recover for a psycho- analytic view that which was closed with the phrase "I have stopped believing in my neurotic patient", that is, lessening the importance of interpersonal determinants.

Returning to Bigliani's text

I made this detour to make it clear that, although I share Bigliani's view that Freud discussed the dimension of the other from the start and that shame is a social feeling which predominantly includes the gaze of the other, this dimension was lost in psychoanalysis for a time.

In this respect, Bigliani shows in his text the different meanings and senses of shame just as they appear in the work of psychoanalytic authors. There is an enormous variety of meanings, but these also show that we are still far from arriving at a definition that is even partly shared.

I list some of the different meanings or senses that are ascribed to shame in the above text.

- Shame is conceived as part of a continuum. It would be the inter- mediate link between mindlessness (the most regressive moment) and the feeling of guilt (the most mature moment) on the road from "invulnerability to vulnerability", from pre-compassion to worry.
- Shame would correspond to a negative assessment of the self.
- Shame is indistinguishable from culpability.
- Shame is a defence against exhibitionism. In this sense, following the text of Freud's *Inhibitions, Symptoms and Anxiety* (Freud, 1926d), there is a distinction between signal shame (operating as an anticipatory function before the emergence of situations where

there might be a paralysing invasion of the ego) and automatic shame (in which the invasion could not be avoided).

- Shame is the expression of the invasion of the ego by an original exhibition of the infantile grandiose self, which would cause "painful shame".
- Shame is associated with identity and narcissistic problems. Along these lines, he emphasises a description of *self narcissism* that would express the evolution of the child towards autonomy and a *narcissism of the object*, in which the child would be subjected to the will of narcissistic parents who would punish with lack of love any transgression of their wishes and who would look upon any differentiation from them (parents) as cruelty. The attempt to differentiate oneself from that symbiotic requirement would cause shame to emerge from an ego that is not mature enough, when seeking to connect with others. "The price of individuation is shame."
- Shame would emerge initially as a signal of a process of differentiation in the face of parental demands and models and, later, with the attempt to grow apart from those demands and models already incorporated with the ego ideal. In the course of treatment, it would be used as an indicator of progress towards individuation.
- Shame is the expression of a forbidden affection, the assumption of a forbidden identity trait, the invasion of the conscience by a fantasy (incestuous, aggressive, exhibitionistic) fit to be repressed by the ego ideal, which rouses a wish to escape regressively towards that ideal to recover the protection granted by undifferentiation, which had been lost in the attempt to grow apart from the parents' wishes or from the ideal. Shame, from this perspective, announces, on the one hand, the attempt to be different, and, on the other, a regressive withdrawal from symbolisation towards the unity (child and parents) of narcissism.
- Shame signals the confession of a defeat, the revelation of a weakness, the loss of appearances and of dignity, which might lead us to imagine our internal world is unveiled in the eyes of the other.

Epilogue

I would like to end my comments by thanking Guillermo Bigliani for the privilege I have had to contribute ideas and suggestions to his text, in this interweaving of the psychoanalytical model and the systemic theory.

Notes

1. If each theory has its own basis of observation, one cannot take into account that which is explained by the other one. It is necessary to make use of a terminology to allow us to say that two theories refer to the same event. This exchange aims precisely at that.
2 . The minutes of the Congress appear in Sluzki, Berenstein, Bleichmar, and Maldonado Allende (1970.)
3. In the origins of psychoanalysis, the effects of the environment were only considered as a reference. In Dora's case history, after Freud had listened to her misadventures involving Mr K´s harassment, and the non-intervention of her father because he was the lover of Mr K´s wife, Freud asked his patient, "What is your role in this story?"

   Freud focuses his research on Dora's psychic reality when he asks that question; he does not pay attention to the effects of the environment. This has clearly been a fertile line of thought in the course of seeking the way in which the intrapsychic conflict develops, but it became an obstacle when it was not understood that this was an instance provided by the framework and it was assumed to be the only causality to be considered when apprehending the emotional life of people (Freud, 1905d). I shall expand on this below.
4. Henry Dicks had, among other merits, that of creating the service for the treatment of couples at the Tavistock Clinic, London, in 1947.
5. Jurg Willi was the Director of the Centre of Psychotherapy in the Psychiatric Hospital that was part of the University of Zurich in the 1970s.
6. In the mid-twentieth century, the USA started to call a child who "charged" against other children intentionally, pursuing and attacking them, "a bully". When several "bullies" form a group or a gang their actions are called "bullying", a verb referring to actions of intimidation and to the abuse of the younger and weaker by the older and stronger children and adolescents.
7. In *Black Mass* (2007), Gray says that lay ideologies, very influential in our times, were forged in the mould of repressed religion, from which they have arisen like versions of the myth of the Apocalypse: believing in an event which will change the world and will put an end to history and all its conflicts.

8. Kaës has studied the idea of Otherness in depth through the "denegative pact" especially in "negativity under obligation". In his conception, what is expelled by the group when the group is instituted goes on to fill a space he calls "a rubbish dump", a site for what has been thrown away, what has been considered part of the Otherness.

9. The notion of "being with another one", whom I admit as different, is a complex idea. I have stated that "we are with another one" only when we admit him as different—and this is not usually the case.

10. It is worth mentioning that the world is what is defined by the Whole. Those who are part of the Otherness are on occasions not granted rights, according to what has been decided by the Whole, which, although different from those of the world, should exist, even if they are despised for being "outside of this world". On other occasions they are expected to be considered by the Whole as non-existent, and when it is impossible to reject their existence and the otherness penetrates what is considered worldly by that world, they arouse feelings of uneasiness in the subjects who are considered worldly.

11. In the case history of Elizabeth von R, where Freud (1895d) advances a step in his comprehension, he changed his mind about the suffering of Ilona Weiss (Elizabeth von R); he thought at first "it was a disappointment after her first love" and went on to understand it as a conflict that involved "her whole moral self".

12. The intuition of a conflict that morally confronts a person is the foundation for Freud's great conceptual leap after his dream about Irma's injection, dreamed by him on 23 July 1895.

    The scene of Emma Eckstein's treatment (Irma), dreamed by Freud, which we now know constitutes the original scene of psychoanalysis, is marked by moral conflicts. When Freud reported and analysed it in the *Traumdeutung*, he voluntarily restricted himself to his professional life; he stressed his own culpability, and this is especially important because we are dealing with his first self-analytical discovery. In Freud's comment we find Emma behind Irma, and this is because Fliess's exculpation is at stake. Fliess's "malpractice" nearly caused Emma to lose her life. Freud absolves himself and, in so far as he identifies himself with his friend, he also absolves him, in spite of his irresponsible professional behaviour.

    Undoubtedly this is part of the story, but it would be naïve to turn Irma—and Emma—simply into victims of two doctors. The story thus recounted eliminates the feminine for the benefit of Freud's relationship with his friend. In order to restore "the feminine", it is necessary to consider the other three women who appear in the dream; it is possible to understand in Freud's associations a fluctuation with regard to his patients: on the one hand, these three women are stupidly reluctant to continue with the treatment; on the other hand, he says, "Women are all the same except for the ideal one". In his search for exculpation in the dream, Freud paints a portrait of a good patient, the ideal one, the one who would accept his solution. What solution did Irma not accept? Freud reproaches her for not having accepted his "solution", "psychical analysis", and the consideration of sexuality it implied. To apprehend "the solution" we must remember that Irma was a young widow. At this point Freud says: "My patient Irma was a young widow; if I wanted to find an excuse for the failure of my treatment I could certainly resort to the fact of her widowhood", thus making a reference to her sexual dissatisfaction. Freud was following a line of thought similar to the one he used with his friend Otto: "He has the habit of giving presents on every possible occasion. Hopefully one day he will find a wife who will make him change his habit". In Freud's opinion, widows and bachelors were prone to having neurotic symptoms, which could be modified through sexual satisfaction.

Some years later, Freud definitely changes his mind. He tells us in a letter to Abraham (09 January 1908), quoted by Appignanesi and Forrester (1992), in response to an interpretation his Berlin friend proposed about the dream of Irma's injection. "Syphilis is not the problem . . . Behind him there is a well-hidden sexual megalomania; the three women are godmothers of my daughters . . . and I love them all!" Abraham had suggested that the associations about trimethylamine led to the suspicion of a syphilitic infection in the patient.

It is not only the sexual desire of a doctor for his attractive women patients, neither is it the wish to relieve their sexual frustration. In his own dream, Freud unveiled sexual desires in a close family network—desires which, if fulfilled, would mean incest.

CHAPTER THREE

Comment II

Carlos E. Sluzki

With a broad pallet of referents and nuances, Bigliani explores in his core chapter many issues, some with a light touch and some more deeply. He takes us on a journey to Freud's family, then to explore anti-Semitism as well as bullying, and finally to share several clinical vignettes—many of them so appealing that they leave us wishing for more. The whole chapter offers us an enlightening introduction to the central subject of this book.

Rather than commenting on many aspects of his discussion, I yield to the temptation of discussing one specific component of the scenario where shame and humiliation takes place. I will also expand a point that he touches on only indirectly, through commentaries such as the one focused on the function of the gaze of the third party. In fact, my comments will be centred on the *witness*, a character who, while less recognised, is a key participant in the plots where shame and humiliation are embedded.

The central dramatic function of the witness is to attest to, and, hence, to give form to, the plot of an event, fixing it in time, in space, and in the narrative sequence.

Let us consider as an example the infamous photographs made public some three years ago of guards and prisoners at the Abu

Ghraib prison in Iraq. As we may recall, they document extremely humiliating and degrading acts carried out by American military personnel on a group of Iraqi prisoners labelled—at least by the jailers—as "the enemy". They show smiling military personnel pointing at a dozen naked prisoners forced to pile up one on top of the other, naked prisoners terrorised by menacing dogs, or being treated themselves as dogs, naked on all fours with a collar, or hooded and connected to false electrodes, or being the object of obviously degrading sexual commentaries by a smiling female guard. Had these photographs *not* been taken in the course of that orgy of humiliation, even if rumours about degrading acts or torture of prisoners would still have circulated, in all likelihood the whole situation would have triggered at the most a routine investigation with little few public repercussions, perhaps including some hand-slapping to quash the accusations of military cruelty (as if the violence of war were a set of actions that could have been contained by the gentleman's agreement of the Geneva Convention!). However, the fact that those photographs were made public transforms those of us who saw those photographs into legitimising witnesses, adding us as accomplices to the dynamics of the social process of humiliation, and adding our voice of indignation in an effort to differentiate us from the perpetrators. Further, those victims were humiliated in extremely asymmetric scenarios, not very different from a situation of "bullying", where the victims lack the resources to confront the perpetrators and reverse the situation or, at the least, redeem themselves through hopeless protestations. This resonates with the prevailing social tendency of witnesses to identify with the victim of any asymmetric violence, facilitating in us an experience of humiliation-by-proxy, that is, placing ourselves in the locus of the victim. This tendency was magnified in this case by the fact that the photograph locates us topographically in the scene as if we were holding the camera, that is, in the amoral position of a photographer–accomplice who, by visually recording those degrading acts, seems to condone them or even to share the pleasure of those actions (as an eroticised witness of a rape). That compels us, the circumstantial witnesses, to differentiate ourselves from that accomplice–photographer–witness, which we do by experiencing and expressing moral indignation. This complex dynamic resonates with Sontag's (2003) suggestion that to look at photographs of atrocities reconstitutes (reminds us of) the moral order, makes us part of the collective consensus of what is good and what is bad, of which action can be labelled as noble and which as evil, in this case through proclamations of sympathy and solidarity for the victims, representing the human rights orientation of the moral order of the Western culture of our times.

As I discuss in more detail in the next chapter, the experience of humiliation is magnified and, in some cases, activated through the presence of this third party, namely, the witness, whether it is close or distant, materially present or internalised, relevant or even unknown.[1] The nature of the experience of a given negative event—whether it is a minor misstep on the pavement, an experience of political torture, or a gang rape—depends in part on the nature of the testimonial presence: the witness helps to define whether the victims' experiences are being echoed by somebody (ultimately, a representative of the moral order of the community) that is either in solidarity with them ("We suffer with you"), indifferent ("That's not my problem"), or perversely segregating ("How ridiculous you look!" "What a coward you are!"). This witnessing might materialise perhaps even as a comment by a perpetrator while also acting as a witness, like a hostile Greek chorus debasing the victim himself (a rapist stating "You like it, you slut!" or a torturer stating "You weakling, you cry and shout over nothing!") (Sluzki, 1993).

This variety of testimonial qualities might induce a broad range of different emotions in the victims of acts or events that may be intrinsically identical. They might go from the profoundly ego-dystonic experience of *humiliation*, when the value judgments of the third parties are experienced by the self as unfair and offensive, to the equally unpleasant but ego-syntonic experience of *shame*, where the emotion is anchored in an attribute of the subject that the subject himself agrees in considering defective or meriting criticism, as clearly exemplified by the vicissitudes of Maria in Bigliani's third vignette.[2]

One of the merits of this differentiation between ego-syntonic and ego-dystonic experiences lies in the fact that *the greater the ego-dystony* of the experience, the greater the tendency of the subject toward action in search of redress or revenge. This is because the source of the criticism or debasement—the affront of the negative value judgment concerning the action or inaction—is perceived as external, while *the more ego-syntonic* the demeaning (assumed or actual) comment or action of the other, the greater will be the passivity of the subject beyond the wish or intent to escape or hide or neutralise his own behaviour, as the location of the source of the injury is perceived by the subject as internal—his own defect, his own negative trait.[3]

The introduction of the *witness* into the scene as a powerful third party adds levels of complexity to the architecture of the situation. Using as an example an event that took place in a historical period already visited by Bigliani, that is, after the *Anschluss*, the annexation of Austria by the German Reich in 1938, we know that the Gestapo did not go into the houses of prominent Austrian Jews to humiliate them. They did not force them, for example, to clean the floor of their own kitchen with soap and a brush. Instead, they herded their victims into the street, or detained them while passing by, and forced them at gunpoint to kneel—dressed as they were, in street clothes, overcoat and hat included—and brush the paving stones of a street in the centre of Vienna, while passers-by would end up surrounding them to witness the spectacle, some gazing with indifference, some laughing and applauding, and some looking at the whole scene in horror but silently. As a result, people that until then had been experienced by the victims as fellow citizens became—or were perceived as—hostile observers, many of them indeed galvanised by their identification with the perpetrators. The intent of those spectacles, photographed originally by the Gestapo for purposes of propaganda, was precisely to seal in a qualitative difference between perpetrators plus a crowd of witnesses and their victims and close off any solidarity. Those acts were part of a process towards what Erickson called "pseudospeciation" (cf. Friedman, 1999), which is defining the "other"—in this case, the Jews—as a non- (i.e., sub)-human species.[4] In turn, the indifference or hostility of the crowd indelibly marked many of the victims of those acts of humiliation as an urgent call for action—either by getting politically involved in clandestine actions or by leaving the country in order to escape from the regime's escalating violence. However, other victims of those acts were demolished by the shame of acquiescing to the orders of those who forced those acts (instead of risking their lives by simply refusing to obey), an experience that, internalised, might have contributed to their inaction and to subsequent deportation and extermination.

As members of a society with a modicum of social integration, the experience of a criticism of our presentation of self in any of its many forms constitutes a sign of deviation that entices us to act so as to neutralise it. In turn, when we witness such a scene between third parties, unless we are allied to the perpetrators or agree with their views, we tend to identify with the victim of the humiliation (we will discuss a "humiliation by proxy" in the next chapter) and our impulse is to express our solidarity with the one being humiliated, reacting *a priori* as if this would be an injustice. But it should be added that, when we witness flagrant acts of violence, such as the scenarios described above, in which we become a witness indirectly, through photographs, films, or even narratives of those events, we also tend to experience shame, either of being a member of the human race, or of the group that committed the atrocity, when not overwhelmed by "survivor's guilt" as mentioned by Bigliani when reminding us of some of Primo Levi's formulations. This shame-as-witness triggers, as mentioned above, an effort to decouple ourselves from the perpetrators, to differentiate ourselves from them through our thoughts or deeds, reflecting a moral judgement that the perpetrators seem to lack. As an aside, the intensity of those feelings, and this juggling of alternative positions in the plot, might be the sources of attraction for melodrama as a literary and media genre. Such melodrama can be seen in the interminable radio and television soap operas, loaded with passion, shame, humiliation, betrayals, and revenge (not unlike Bigliani's second vignette), habitually broadcast in the afternoon so that many housewives marooned at home can vicariously replenish their emotion-starved life, as well as in the many Italian operas that draw in their avid public with intensity and passion.

When we become victims of a violation of the social order, the absence of an empathic third party who may witness our suffering and perhaps intercede on our behalf triggers alarms that are filo- and ontogenetically associated with the terror of being ostracised, that is, of social shunning.[5] In fact, the punishment for violations of the social order does not differ whether we are defined as *bona fide* victims or as provocateurs of the perpetration (and, hence, pseudo-victims): we will be expelled from the paradise of the tribe or clan or whatever niche of the social world we belong to. That risk of expulsion or excommunication exists regardless of whether we consider ourselves partly to blame, totally innocent victims, naïve patsies, or scheming co-perpetrators: the presence of a witness, even more an empathic one, is essential for our absolution. The narrative that might label the threat of expulsion as a punishment for our transgressions or imperfections, or as a trick of an arbitrary God who operates with a logic or design that escapes us ("God works in mysterious ways!"), or the product of a misunderstanding, or an unfair act of others, will be contingent on the testimonial narrative produced by, or attributed by us to, *the witness*, whether that position is occupied by a friendly witness who will not blame us and will intercede on our behalf, an indifferent or pusillanimous one who refuses to get involved, a holier-than-thou righteous one who will feel purer by means of defining others as impure, or a contemptuous enemy, who takes pleasure in our suffering while defining us as responsible for our own expulsion. (More on witnessing will be found in the next chapter.)

Many variables contribute to set up the plot, to distribute roles, and to attribute meanings in the myriad of minor or major episodes that might evoke shame or humiliation. One particular modulator derives from our prior life experiences, translated into steady inter-nalised narratives, in turn the result of the fit or misfit between char-acterological proclivities and repetitive experiences of our infancy and childhood. This modulator contributes to building extremely distinct realities, with drastically different consequences such as whether we will end up stuck in the role of victim, witness, or perpetrator in a given episode.

Needless to say, a minority among us will openly acknowledge our role when we happen to occupy the social position of *perpetrators* of the suffering of others (whether in a minor social event or in one with major consequences). However, most of us will reorganise reality (that is, will re-"punctuate the sequence of events", using Watzlawick, Beavin, and Jackson's (1967) terms) so as to be able to occupy the socially neutral position of distracted ("Ooops!"), detached ("That's not my business"), or passionate *witness* ("Oh, what an injustice!"), or the socially ingratiating, and, hence, generally socially safer, position of *victim*. If everything else fails, of course, we can always resort to pleading the role of mere bureaucratic automaton ("It wasn't in my power to avoid it"), a mere cog in a larger machine, as Eichmann por-trayed himself (Arendt, 1961.)

We are immersed in these narrative flows throughout our personal and professional life. Knowing about their dynamics, and, as profes-sionals, being able to maintain the socially responsible position of empathic witness, sensitive to the suffering of others, while varying in our professional responsibility to destabilise those narratives so as to increase ethical alternative realities, allows us to retain a reasonable sense of (temporary, insecure, requiring permanent vigilance) citizenship as members of the human family.

Notes

1. Several patients I have treated who, as political prisoners, were victims of torture, said that while they were being tortured, usually blindfolded, they were trying to figure out *who else* was present in the torture chamber in addition to the torturer: if nobody else was there, they said, the experience ended up being somehow more tolerable, less humiliating. This will be exemplified in one of the clinical vignettes in Chapter Four of this book.

2. I intentionally chose a phenomenological and interactive (witness-based) reading of the experience of humiliation in order to challenge the assumption that the dynamic of humiliation has a point of departure that is necessarily intrapersonal, an assumption that might obfuscate descriptions about the causation of those processes that I wish to highlight. In this regard, see also Scheff (2000) and Volkan (2004), as well as a very interesting critical review of Volkan's 2004 book by Scheff (2004.)

3. Carlos, the main character of Bigliani's first vignette, does not experience shame for excluding his father because he is speaking on behalf of his mother, rather than as a third party. The therapeutic endeavour of differentiating his self from the collective therefore will become more cumbersome, as the road towards achieving it will confront him with the painful experience of the irruption of shame, as will be discussed in Chapter Four.

4. "The moral witness—be it the person who is suffering or only an observer of the pain that derives from malignant actions—must himself assume a personal risk" (Margalit, 2002, p. 150). And those were extremely dangerous times to dissent.

5. Imagine a tragic scene in which a mother is hitting a child who, terrorised, runs towards her and hugs her as a refuge, crying "Mummy!" not as a placating ploy, but as an enactment of disassociated roles, or even as a call for the mother to rematerialise as such, as the child is escaping from the beater, who is leaving him alone and defenceless, towards the security of her embrace.

CHAPTER FOUR

Humiliation, shame, and associated social emotions: a systemic approach and a guide for its transformation

Carlos E. Sluzki

A struggling composer living in a minuscule, dark tenement apartment with his wife and his ailing father, barely surviving on the tips he earns while playing the piano in a dingy bar, has a chance to submit a symphonic piece of his own to the legendarily temperamental conductor of the city's prestigious philharmonic orchestra. To his surprise, the director, after studying the score, informs him that not only will he première his composition with the city's orchestra, but that he would like the composer to conduct his own piece as part of a full gala concert otherwise led by the orchestra's regular conductor. Overjoyed, the young composer runs home and shares the good news with his wife and father, filled with joy: success is within his reach.

The day of the concert has arrived. As they are leaving their apartment, a good friend of theirs who is escorting them to the opera house reminds the man to take with him the tailcoat that, as director of his piece, the composer is supposed to wear in a gala concert. The composer looks at his friend dumbfounded: he hasn't even thought of that. He is overcome with despair until his wife, her face beaming with relief, remembers that a few days ago she saw a tailcoat in the display window of a nearby Salvation Army clothing store.

While he goes to the concert hall, she rushes to the store and, exhausting their last savings, buys the tailcoat without even taking the time to check its size. She rushes to the concert hall, arriving a few minutes before the concert begins, to everybody's relief. With considerable effort, and just in time for his call, the composer-turned-conductor manages to put on the jacket, obviously tailored for a man rather smaller than his slightly rotund figure.

The regular conductor of the orchestra accompanies him to the podium, introduces him warmly to the audience, all dressed in gala attire, as expected, and leaves.

After the audience gives him some courtesy applause, the composer steps on to the podium and, at the signal from his baton, the orchestra begins the concert under his rather impassionate conduction All goes well until, as he gesticulates vigorously, his too-tight tailcoat begins to tear apart at the seams, first subtly, but then rather obviously. A gesture to the double-bass players, and the seams that hold the centre of the back of the jacket give up. A gesture to the piccolo, and there go the seams of the right sleeve. The progressive destruction of the tailcoat proceeds inexorably while the conductor, oblivious to it all, continues directing his piece.

At this spectacle, which seems like a slapstick routine, the audience begins to giggle and then to laugh aloud. The composer continues directing for a while, increasingly distressed, without understanding what is going on, until the first violin stands up, approaches him, and whispers in his ear what is happening. The composer, startled, stops directing, reaches around to his back, only to confirm that the sleeves of the tailcoat have detached. By then the orchestra has stopped playing, while the audience continues to laugh. The composer turns around, looks at the audience with rancour, then tears off his tailcoat and throws it to the floor, climbs off the podium and, shifting his mood, sits on it, hides his face in his hands, and begins to cry.

The audience, in obvious discomfort or even embarrassment, shifts from laughter to awkward murmuring, until total silence ensues: the revered regular conductor of the philharmonic orchestra, standing up sternly in the proscenium, has taken off his own tailcoat and states in his strong, resonant voice, "Please, maestro, continue." The audience, moved by the gesture, explodes in thunderous applause for the maestro, while all the men proceed to take off their own jackets. The applause of the audience and of the orchestra brings the composer back from his well of despair. He first looks around in disbelief. Then, still shaken but recomposing himself, stands up while the applause continues and, this time jacketless, slowly climbs back to the podium from where, at a signal from his baton, the orchestra continues playing what is clearly going to be a triumphant debut.[1]

Several moments of this very moving—while slightly corny—story merit highlighting, using as a lens the emotion dynamics we are discussing:

First, in the transition that starts when the main character, still puzzled by the laughter of the audience, ceases conducting and realises that his jacket is disintegrating, he displays in sequence two closely connected but very distinct emotions: his hateful stare at the audience denotes an experience of *humiliation*, where the source of the experience is external ("You miserable people, laughing at me, denigrating my work through your pettiness, robbing me of a triumph that was within reach!"), while his shift to covering his face and crying shows him hunched in *shame*, the source of the experience internalised in part as a self-reproach ("Swallow me, earth! I have created my own failure!") or as fate ("I always have such bad luck!").

Second, his public display of shame, an emotion habitually hidden or, at most, expressed only in intimate settings, "humanises" the composer in the eyes of the public, who react by showing increasing discomfort—*guilt*—due to the suffering that their laughter and scorn has caused.

Third, the stern look of the highly respected regular orchestra conductor disassociates him from the rest of the audience, and makes him a *critical witness* that defines the audience's laughter as contemptible.

Fourth, at the same time, the noble gesture of the orchestra maestro acts as a catalytic agent, as it offers a way out: the audience, until that moment not knowing what to do to reduce its own growing distress, identifies with the reparatory, solution-based behaviour modelled by the conductor and join him, in an effort to dissolve the collective guilt with their enthusiastic applause. This latter scene also illustrates the powerful impact that a charismatic leader (when appearing at the right moment) has on a distressed crowd in search of a dignified exit, as well as the relief provided by a strong act of symbolic *request for forgiveness in turn granted* by the composer by continuing his performance (rather than, for instance, leaving the stage, offended, which would have been understood as a refusal of the apology). Of course, this sequence also assures him a standing ovation at the end, regardless of the intrinsic quality of his composition, as the public will experience relief and express appreciation for the composer's acceptance of their apology and dismissal of the unpleasant episode.

Introduction

The complex task of living in society requires us to be permeable to the opinions and expectations of the other members of the collective of which we are a part. (Reciprocally, we assume that they will be sensitive to our own opinions and expectations.) These assumptions allow us to programme, evaluate, and refine our social actions on the basis of how they will impact on others, thus helping us to calibrate our relationship with the surrounding social world, helping us to establish and maintain relationships, reducing the risk of destabilising them, and, if needed, pinpointing and managing agreements or disagreements involving assumptions. Furthermore, we are capable of heightening or reducing our sensitivity to others' signals contingent on the relative power or value of the actors: we heighten that sensitivity *vis-à-vis* people to whom we wish to signal our esteem or respect: our true love, a powerful chief, a sovereign. We might also choose to inform our view of our relative position of strength and power by acting less sensitively with subordinates, people lower on the totem pole, or weaker in one way or another.[2] It should be noted that, far from being a trait exclusive to human beings, this social ability appears in many other mammals for whom group life is essential for survival.

Most of these processes do not take place as a machination, but at a preconscious level to which we have access only if and when we focus our attention on them, or when emotions pass a certain threshold and demand our attention. To be a part of a social world requires that we should be neither excessively impermeable nor excessively permeable to our own emotions, as well as to signals or opinions or expectations of others, that is, neither impervious to them nor slaves to them, but to be accurate interpreters of signals that emanate from within or from without. These processes are central for establishing, maintaining, and changing interpersonal relations, establishing or challenging hierarchies, and other behaviours equally aimed at "living and letting live" in society. This subtle balance between identity and sociality varies from circumstance to circumstance, from person to person, and from context to context; moreover, it constitutes a trait that differentiates one person from the next. For instance, a personal style located at the "impervious" extreme of the spectrum of "permeability" will tend to be labelled as arrogant or insensitive, while one characterised by traits of the "hyper-sensitive" end will be considered over-sensitive, insecure, submissive, or dependent.

In order to maintain this equilibrium between these and other extremes, we rely on emotional signals that function in tight association with our neuro-endocrine system, collaborating in the prediction, evaluation, and calibration of our performance in terms of their social effect so as to reduce its alarm signals. They are a set of pleasant or unpleasant emotions, sensations, and experiences that have been aggregated under the label of *social emotions*, which are self-referential sensitivities that facilitate adjustment between our view of ourselves and of others in the social context, and, therefore, of our behavioural adaptation or challenges in the process of social insertion. In fact, in our forecast of scenes from the immediate and mediate future, the nature of these emotions will entice us to select behaviours aimed at avoiding or, at least, hiding, those that are predicted as having negative consequences, and maximizing those that lead to positive consequences.[3] To repeat what has been noted above already, a good part of the process takes place outside the awareness of the individual—that is, unconsciously—and the social emotions that we might experience are but the "tip of the iceberg."

Traits such as interpersonal sensitivity, empathy, and "social intelligence" have been explored from the vantage point of biology, psychology, social construction, and positions in the discourse. I am quick to confess that I shall indulge in the sin of eclecticism during the treatment of these themes, as I shall choose one or another of those constructs depending on which will seem to have, for me at the moment, a greater descriptive or explanatory power.

You, reader, as a subject . . . and researcher

May I ask you, reader, to perform *now*, at this very moment, a five-step exercise? I hope that you will accept, and that you will find both process and outcome interesting.

1. Reader, please stop reading for a moment and find, if you please, a couple of blank pages, or a notebook, and also a pen or a pencil—you may use your computer instead, if you have it handy. *Do it now.* Next, please try and remember an incident in which you have participated that remains in your memory because *you felt humiliated.* You may start, if need be, by remembering an experience that left you outraged or at least offended, a frequent hint of the emotion of humiliation. *Do it now.*

2. Once you have captured that moment, kindly record it in writing, in some detail. You should fill no less than half a page. Once you have done it, you may resume reading. *Do it now.*

3. Once you have finished writing your notes, please choose a CD. If you have an iPod® handy, or music archived in your computer, that will do. Find a piece of music that you particularly enjoy, and listen to it for a couple of minutes, comfortably relaxed. (I should confess that this step is designed only to distract you and perhaps yank you away from possible unpleasant memories triggered by this last exercise!) *Do it now.*

4. Now, for the next task, please recall an incident you took part in that remains in your memory as a situation in which you, willingly or unwillingly, *humiliated somebody else.*

5. Once you have captured that moment, kindly write it down with some detail on a different piece of paper or page of the notebook, covering no less than half a page. *Do it now.*

You have now completed your "fieldwork", which consisted of the recall and recording of autobiographical material. You have in front of you two narratives, one in which the central character (the informant, namely, you) has been involved in a scene or situation in which s/he felt humiliated, and another in which that same person perceived him/herself as the perpetrator of humiliation on another person. In other words, leaving aside the details of the plot, which usually includes description of contexts that frame the behaviour or emotions of the participants, in the first vignette the informant was in the social position of victim and in the second, that of perpetrator.

Almost covertly, I would like to ask you a question: which one of the two stories was more uncomfortable to describe or write? Which of the two social positions, that of victim and that of perpetrator, was more unpleasant to recall? Once you have answered those questions for yourself, you should know that, unless the situation evoked was egregious, the majority of people who answered those questions find it more tolerable to recall situations in which they occupied the social position of victim than that of perpetrator. And it is not surprising, as the position of victim has several social advantages when compared to that of perpetrator. We shall return to this issue later in this chapter.

Let us now proceed to analysing comparatively the two narratives you have in front of you.

We shall begin by exploring the *content of the plot*. To facilitate your analysis, you may utilise these categories:

- broken promises;
- lies discovered;
- rules violated;
- secrets unveiled;
- oppressive, arbitrary power ploys;
- betrayals of one type or another.

Around which categories were the plots of your stories of victimisation woven (in each of the two roles)? Granted, there is no statistical tool, however powerful and discriminating, that will permit a solid correlation between "themes" and "position in the plot" with an $n=2$, with a sample of only two narratives. However, you might find it interesting to know that an analysis of responses from a statistically meaningful sample of respondents has shown a lack of correlation between plot theme and position of the narrator: neither people recalling stories in which they were in a position of victims nor of perpetrators showed a thematic preference.[4] However, perhaps you will find something of personal interest by observing the themes you have chosen . . . or perhaps not.

Let us proceed now to explore any differences that you might notice in the plot and/or in the words you choose to use in your stories. When narratives focused on these positions are analysed in *structural* and *semantic* terms in larger samples, the differences between the two stories is remarkable. Perhaps you will notice, as we have found in our own research, a clear discrepancy between elements of the stories in which you were a victim and those where you were the perpetrator: they show differences in terms of *intensity* attributed to the emotion, the *duration* of the impact, and the *explanatory context* of the transgression. Broadly speaking, we tend to express more indignation and justice seeking when we are victims, while being more generous and explanatory about our own behaviour when we are perpetrators. More specifically, stories in which the informants define themselves as *victims* of acts or circumstances accentuate the negative consequence, the damage to the relationship, the arbitrary nature of the motivations of the perpetrator, the unjustified, immoral, intentional, impulsive, or cruel aspect of those behaviours, with more details about the preliminary moves that led to the act, and showing signs that the wound has not totally healed but could even now ooze a remnant of anger. As perpetrators, in turn, people tend to describe the incident more sparsely, defining them as atypical or circumstantial, and their histories include reparation, self-blame, forgiveness, and closure, with a happy ending of sorts, including displeasure for having behaved as humiliators while offering some mitigating circumstances or a reference to having been provoked, as well as criticism of the other for having over-reacted or exaggerated their humiliation. With those tendencies in mind, dear reader, please compare your two narratives and explore whether you detect in them any of these differences . . . or whether you are the exception to the rule, an outlier in the distribution curve.

Your research project ends here. I hope you found it interesting and even enlightening. Let us now return to the main thrust of this chapter. (If you find it helpful, you might want to use some of your responses as examples as pertinent themes are discussed.)

The construction of a shared reality and the struggle for privileged positions

Conflicting narratives of social violence inhabited by perpetrators, victims, and witnesses constitute fascinating arenas where struggles for the privileged positions within the narratives take place. They frequently evolve as "memory wars", where the legitimacy of each individual (in the micro-world of a couple) or ideological group's "official story" (in the meso-world of institutions as well as in the macro-world of international relations) is legitimised, tested, and contested.[5] And narratives that contain violence in one form or another tend to be firmly held, as they draw from, and remind us of, what is

and should be considered acceptable or unacceptable (political parameters), good and bad (ethic parameters), good and evil (moral, and
not infrequently religion-based, judgements), and even about what
constitutes a credible reality, regardless of tangible evidence.

The Crusades tend to be described in novels and in films as epic
stories that trace the sagas of noblemen—generally third or fourth in
the line of succession in their own house and therefore with meagre
chances of inheriting their father's estates and positions—guided by
their wish to rescue the Holy Sites from the hands of infidels. They
tend to be portrayed as generous as well as fierce, fair, and valiant.
However, in the counter-stories that were transmitted (and embell-
ished) from generation to generation by the victims of the pillages,
looting, rapes, and indiscriminate killings that characterised their
passage through any territory deemed unholy, they were vile, ignorant, heartless, and violent individuals, to the point that the word
"crusade", lightly used by a previous president of the USA to label
rhetorically the invasion of Iraq, triggered a collective reaction of
indignation among Muslims, for whom that word connoted brutal
experiences that their population suffered during that period of history. And there are still more counter-stories that detail the ferocious
treatment of those vanquished by the Muslim armies of both the Cali-
phate and the Ottoman Empire.

In the USA, the bloody Civil War of 1861–1865 that pitted the
northern industrial states against the southern agricultural states was
triggered by the decision of the federal government—with a majority
of representatives from the north—to abolish slavery. It was won, as
we know, by the armies of the Union, that is, by the northern states.
That war is generally described by citizens raised in the Northern
states as a historic event, lodged in the remote past, while it remains
in the lore of most people raised in the South as a very present humiliating defeat, a source of resentment and, in many cases prejudice
against "those damn Yankees".[6]

These vignettes could easily have been replaced by contrasting
stories of Muslims and Hindus in Bangladesh or Kashmir, or Hutus
and Tutsis in Rwanda, or Serbs, Croats, and Bosnians in the former
Yugoslavia, or of parties on either side of the hundreds of local,
regional, and global wars that desolated and still desolate many
regions of this world, with the story favoured by the winners becoming the "official story". In fact, the contrasting construction of the

narratives of victimisation by those who define themselves as victims (the vast majority of those narratives) or as perpetrators (generally justified by a previous victimisation, as their story goes) is at the core of many interpersonal, institutional, and international disputes (Lindner, 2006; Scheff, 2000). We shall return to this theme later.

We may advance here the notion that the destabilisation and deconstruction of conflicting stories and the generation of alternative, complementary rather than confrontational narratives is at the centre of narrative-based approaches to therapy as well as to mediation or conflict resolution, aiming at dislodging those stories that anchor shame and/or humiliation in the parties, redistributing responsibilities, and increasing the possibility of redress, reparations, or transcendence. While the steps of the process that goes from conflict to reconciliation will not be discussed, as it is a topic less relevant to the subject at hand (and is described elsewhere (Sluzki, 2010)), this chapter will focus on analysing the narrative anchoring of these emotions, and the way these emotions increase the tenacity of those narratives.

Social emotions

To start with, I will revisit what has been proposed in prior pages, using a slightly different language. There is within each of us an unstable equilibrium between (a) our experience of personal identity, that is, our self, displaying a reasonable degree of coherence between values, ethics, and behaviour and over time, and (b) our view of our meaningful others' view of us, tied to our drive towards sociality, our attachments, and, hence, our relative dependence on the other. In fact, our identity might be the result of what Laing, Phillipson, and Lee (1966) called the "spiral of reciprocal perspectives": my image of you, my image of your image of me, my image of your image of my image of you, and so on, in sequence. This double process, entailing introspection as well as projection (or assumptions), replicated endlessly among those who surround us, constitutes our identity-in-society, in which the others' behaviours are cause and effect of many of our own behaviours. These spirals include not only those who are part of our meaningful personal social network, but even the anonymous others, potential witnesses of our actions and our vicissitudes. In fact, that also holds true when we become a witness of their vicissitudes and even witnessing our own being a witness: think, for instance, of that flood of solidarity in distress that invaded you the first time you saw that now famous photograph of a Vietnamese girl running naked down an almost deserted road while screaming in pain and terror, her body blistered by napalm.[7]

Our virtues (and sometimes our defects) need to be recognised by key witnesses. If we are our own solid witness, we might not need another person's eye, but we risk drifting into an anomic world. In some cases we may also want to (need to) be rejected or criticised by those witnesses whose approval would place us in an alliance with those whom we repudiate. This process is steered, at one level, by our cognition (our socio-political mind, informed by our lived life and our values) and, at another, by a set of *social emotions*, both positive or pleasurable and negative or unpleasant, that calibrate our behaviours, informing us about the approval (or prediction of approval) or rejection (or its risk) by Others, calibrating the proximity or distance between the way we want to be/appear and the way we are (or might be) perceived by the Others.

From this set of emotions we will select for this analysis those that are labelled as *negative*, that is, those associated with social situations we try to avoid or, if they occur, to neutralise or change. The "negative" label has two referents: they are unpleasant or uncomfortable experiences, the stick rather than the carrot enticement to change, and they generate what in cybernetics is called "negative feedback", that is, they elicit behaviours aimed at correcting the deviation that triggered the alarm.

Negative social emotions[8]

As implied above, negative social emotions are self-referential (centred in the self) while social in their origin. (They require the presence of at least one other person, and two characters, as we shall discuss later in this chapter.[9]) They signal the disparity between how we want to be perceived and judged and how we believe we are perceived and judged in a given context, when this disparity may lead to the degradation of the image that the Other has (or could have) of us, which in turn contains the potential for reducing the quality of our self-image and, hence, of our self-esteem.

To start with a mild negative social emotion, *social discomfort or embarrassment* is a kind of "minor shame", an experience (or risk) of temporary disapproval of our image or of esteem on the part of the Other (and, hence, on our own self-image and self-esteem). It may take place, for example, as a result of a social *faux pas*, and it tends to be easily erased through an explanation ("I known this may not be the ideal attire, but I had to work late, and I came as I was in order not to arrive late"), an apology (a "Sorry" after burping), or an explicit recognition of the deviant behaviour in front of the other (an "Ooops!" while closing a zipper inadvertently left unzipped), or even a denial of the whole situation (such as acting as if nothing had happened after passing wind in public with a small sound).

The list also includes two more intense aversive social emotions, *shame* and *humiliation*, which have in common the sense of being discovered and devalued or dishonoured publicly on the basis of acts that we have committed or omitted. Despite this common trait, they present an important difference: *shame* takes place when there is an *agreement* between the criticism by the public eye and our own, that is, becomes unchained when the loss of social worth in the other's image of us (or at least our image of their image of us) coincides with our own devaluation of our behaviour-in-context, while *humiliation* is experienced when the negative image of us that we attribute to, or is manifested by, the other *does not concur* with our view of the circumstances or event or appropriateness of the denunciation or with our assumptions or description of our behaviour by the other; therefore, we experience the other's behaviour or assumptions inappropriate and our degradation by them unfair.

While we will explore in detail those differences, it is not always easy to distinguish between the two, as it is frequently contingent upon our "taking sides" with one or another description or attribution or characters in the story, while both can coexist under certain circumstances. We may feel humiliated, for instance, by the contemptuous behaviour of a given individual *vis-à-vis* ourselves and ashamed that others might have witnessed that situation. Our humiliation is even greater if we did not react as we wished, for instance, with indignation, hence accepting the other's derogatory definition of us.

To the list of negative social emotions we may add *guilt*, an experience that is more focalised than shame. It is generally triggered by personal acts or lack of action that may have hurt or inconvenienced the other, risking having somehow damaged the relationship. However, the damage is deemed to be reparable through apology, compensation, or some ritual form of self-punishment, leading potentially to forgiveness (by the other) and at least to self-forgiveness ("I am a good person who made a mistake and is trying to correct it."). In fact, guilt, because of its social value as a stimulant of corrective actions, protects the self against the more prolonged and deleterious experience of shame. Needless to say, when the damage is impossible to repair (e.g., while driving under the influence, we turned on to the road without paying attention and crashed our car into a van, killing the three children of a family that was driving by), we may carry our guilt throughout life, as a heavy load. We may purge it through self-sacrifice (devoting our life to nursing in a leper colony, for instance) or avoid it by committing suicide.

It can be said, then, that *guilt* is the emotion that accompanies our belief that we did something wrong, *shame* emerges when believing (publicly or at least in front of our judging self) that we are, somehow, bad, and *humiliation* emerges when, regardless of whether we did something wrong by commission or omission or even by being bad, we are being unfairly debased by the other. Let us explore the two latter emotions in more detail.

Shame, as mentioned above, is an emotion tied to seeing oneself in a negative light through the eyes of the other, or anticipating that possibility. According to self-perception, that negative view or critical perception by the other(s) or by ourselves is justified. Shame, perhaps in interplay with its polar opposite, *pride*, is one of the emotional axes that organise interpersonal relations (Scheff, 2000; Scheff & Retzinger, 1991a,b). Thus, shame traps the individual, at least momentarily, in a future tinted by that failure, instilling a sense of reduced self-value and of self-rejection that tends to be experienced at the moment as irreversible. Self is perceived as an inferior, defective subject, lacking any action that could erase the effect of the misdeed.

In the social scenario of shame, the focus is centred on the experience—and the behaviours or omissions—of the *shamed one*: the person who experiences shame does so because of his flawed attributes or behaviours. Victims (or witnesses) may criticise perpetrators for being too severe or careless in exposing their (the victim's) flaws, but the shamed person focuses his attention, and assumes that others do, too, on the imperfection of his own self mainly *because at that moment the shamed person agrees with the criticism.* There is, indeed, an increased risk of being exposed to shame in interactions with a person whose judgement we value, or who is in a position of power over us (echoes of parent–child relations), as well as in public more than in private (that is, without, rather than in front of, witnesses).

An iterated and/or massive experience of shame may be the prelude to two vicious interpersonal cycles: shame ←→ abuse (which reconstitutes shame and the experiences of self-contempt and fear, reducing the ability to defend self, and increasing isolation), and shame ←→ failure (as shame inhibits the efficiency of future actions, along the lines of Seligman's (1975) "learned helplessness.").[10] The anticipation of that possibility, associated with the fear of social isolation, is at the core of the social function of anticipated shame. Paradoxically, this emotion generates the impulse to hide, to disappear from the scene where it took place ("Swallow me, earth!").[11]

In turn, *humiliation*[12] may be defined as the emotion that denounces a situation in which we are (or assumed to be) *unfairly* treated in a negative or demeaning fashion by the other, or anticipating the possibility that our self has been unfairly debased, especially in front of witnesses, as we shall discuss later. Opposite emotions range from the benign experience of being appreciated and respected to the more maligned one of pride (cf. endnote 18). As implied by its polar opposite emotion, humiliation is associated with an experience of attack against dignity, pride, or power, and triggers motions (actions or at least fantasies) of retaliation or revenge (Figure 4.1).

In scenarios of humiliation, the behaviours, attributes, and intentions of (or attributed to) the *perpetrator* are at the centre of the critical discourse of the humiliated, rather than his/her own traits.

Hence, it can be said that one of the important differences between these emotions is that *we would like to forget* the experience of shame as well as those situations where we have experienced them, while we vividly *retain in our memory* the situations where we have been humili-

EMOTION→	←SOCIAL CONCERN→	←(RE)ACTION
Discomfort	Disapproval	"Cancelling"
Guilt	Damage to the relationship	Reparation
Shame	Social isolation	Escape/hide
Humiliation	Loss of dignity/power	Anger/revenge

Figure 4.1. Emotions, social concerns, and (re)actions.

ated. Sometimes, we do so in order to keep our distance from the mistrusted or dangerous perpetrator, sometimes expecting and even planning to exact retribution or revenge if and when the occasion arises (unless, of course, we have disqualified and dismissed the perpetrator and his/her views as worthless, or we decide to forgive him/her).

Needless to say, the boundaries between social emotions are permeable, and grey zones between them can be fairly frequently found. One may, for instance, experience shame due to a *faux pas* that one committed and that elicited disdain from another person, but feel humiliated at the same time due to that person's public display of his/her reaction. A more complex and macabre example follows.

In the course of the recent Balkan wars, as the Serbian armed forces invaded neighbouring Bosnia-Herzegovina, they implemented a systematic policy of massacring men and male children, usually defenceless peasants, as well as collective raping of women and female children, not infrequently done in the presence of one another, and of their husbands and fathers, who were contained at gunpoint. Beyond justifying those rapes as an effort to "contaminate the genetic pool of others" by impregnating women belonging to another ethnic or religious community, the intent of those acts was to destroy the moral fibre of that population by forcing them to be victims as well as witnesses to those egregious acts. The men were unable to defend "their" women and women were unable to protect their female children from the assaults. For a while, the dominant emotion that remained in that population was shame—in women because of their impotence to defend themselves against that outrage to their body and their modesty, compounded by the barrage of deprecatory comments by the perpetrators. The surviving men blamed themselves for having been unable to prevent the attacks. However, those acts remained in the collective memory and were transformed into humiliation. This fed not only efforts at regional autonomy and resistance against post-war reconciliation but, even more seriously, could remain for centuries as seeds of potential wars of revenge.[13]

Shame and humiliation as social compass

Shame and humiliation (either the actual emotions or their prediction) operate, then, as one of those rudders that guide our insertion into the social world, informing us about how our behaviours are, or could be, perceived by others, how much dissonance or consonance there is between our ways and the rules of the relationship, the social circumstances, and the culture surrounding us. The more supple the relationship between our own expectations, the signals we receive from the social world, our own personal ethical norms, and the circumstantial priorities of the social context, the more these social emotions will operate as useful markers to navigate the ever-changing waters of the social world. If, instead, these emotions acquire ubiquitous dominance regardless of context, we will become their terrorised servants, oppressed by an endless set of immobilising rules that will flood our self, clouding our evaluation of the context and of ourselves-in-context, generating high levels of suffering both subjectively and/or in those who populate our surrounding social world.

Shame, an emotion that is also at times anticipatory and at times reactive, constitutes, in fact, a key guide for sociality and even for morality. It is a gyroscope that signals possible transgressions—both past, as a learning experience, and future, as an alarm signal—and, therefore, acts as a prelude, if not as a key component, of what we call conscience. As it emerges from elemental situations that threaten our self-image, shame contains a potential threat to the stability of relationships, and constitutes an important resource for preventing or detecting and mending relational problems. Among its many effects, it contributes to the social regulation of the expression of emotions, because it operates as a filter that reduces the impulsive or uncontrolled expression of feelings—anger, fear, love—that, if enacted each time they emerge, would run against standard social practices in most, if not all, societies and cultures. Regardless of its utility, however, whenever shame acquires a dominant role in the world view of the individuals, it has the effect of ruining their self-esteem, as it inhibits their capacity to act, that is, their "voice", condemning them to dangle like puppets from what they perceive as a tight web of stringent social rules.

Some forms of shame elicited in complex scenarios merit mention as well. Such is the case of *empathic shame*, which emerges when we identify emotionally with people who might be involved in a situation that may have generated shame in them (such as witnessing a pianist who, during a recital, stops in the middle of a performance, clearly having forgotten how the piece he was interpreting continues),[14] and of the *shame by abdication of the self*, a shame–guilt combination that emerges when we observe ourselves critically for not having done whatever we consider that we *should* have done (not confessing to our distracted Year 2 teacher that we were the one who threw a piece of chalk, leading to a punishment for the whole class; not having jumped on the grenade that was thrown into our foxhole to absorb the impact of its explosion and so save our comrades, as one of them did).

As was the case with shame, humiliation also accomplishes important emotional and social functions. Humiliation externalises responsibility, as it defines the subject as a victim of an injustice perpetrated by the other, thus defining both the source and the responsibility as external to the self. In that way, the good standing and honour of the individual, threatened by what is defined as the unjust enactment of the other, is protected, and, further, it promotes actions aimed at countering that move through retaliation of some kind. From that viewpoint, it is an emotion that favours social change at a micro- (relational) or macro social level as it focuses the attention not on the subject, but on components of the relationship or the context that need to be redressed. It is not surprising that, as a consequence, this emotion favours enactment of revenge and violence, with all its potentially destructive consequences.

The social advantages of the victim position

Real life circumstances tend to lead the participants into competing descriptions of the sequence and nature of the events and therefore contradictory descriptions of the roles and of the very nature of the situation: "It's your fault!" "No, it's yours!" "You started it!" "No, *you* did!", also portrayed by the classic, "I withdraw because you nag"; "No, I nag because you withdraw!" with which Watzlawick, Beavin, and Jackson (1967) exemplify the struggle for alternative "punctuations of the sequence of events". These competing descriptions establish where (and by whom) a sequence was initiated, and, therefore, who is victim, who is perpetrator, and, sometimes, who is a witness, and is the basis of countless quarrels between couples, inter-institutional squabbles, and international conflicts. In the realpolitik of life, this struggle among participants tends to aim at acquiring the *socially privileged position of being the victim*.

The social locus of victim tends to evoke in third parties *social solidarity and empathy*, commiseration for their plight and displays of allegiance and alliance with the victim as well as distance from the perpetrator. In meso- and macro-social situations, an added desirable effect is that it creates a community among those who are defined as co-victims (a variation on "My enemy's enemies are my friends"). It should be clarified that the "third parties" mentioned above can be direct eye-and-ear witnesses or people involved through open or secret connection, rumour, media, or other public displays, from singular and expressive sources of testimony to the very abstract "public eye".

A stance of victimhood enacts an *externalisation of responsibility*. It establishes for the victim the illusion of impunity through providing a socially acceptable argument for the display of acts of retaliation, including violence against those defined as, or associated with, the perpetrators. This is even truer when those acts are sanctioned and even expected in our culture. In fact, in patriarchal honour-based cultures, flagrant acts of violence are justified when they are labelled as revenge, even if the acts that the victim labelled as humiliating and "justified" the revenge were part of a symmetrical escalation in which each party defined their behaviour as a reaction to a prior affront by the other (see, e.g., Dershowitz, 1994). This results in endless sequences of reciprocal revenge between family and organisational clans in many areas of the globe and is the occasional prelude to disastrous military conflagrations within or between countries. It also appears as an argument to justify the murder of "unfaithful wives" by a humiliated husband whose honour has been deemed stained by her betrayal.

These social advantages explain the tenacity of the narratives of victimisation (frequently reciprocal, each party stubbornly defining the other as the perpetrator and self as the victim), and the difficulties in helping them evolve those stories towards more flexible narratives of personal responsibility and reciprocal recognition of rights, transformations that, when they take place, open up the path toward reconciliation (Sluzki, 2010).

A caveat must be added: experiences of extreme humiliation—including being victims of repeated violence, such as rapes, torture, and detention in appalling conditions. such as a concentration camp—may elicit utter shame in the victims, even if they themselves may label that emotion as unfair, "absurd", and "paradoxical at a rational level", as Primo Levi asserted (Levi, 1989, pp. 73, 77; see also Cien-fuegos & Monelli, 1983; Hayner, 2002; Shapiro, 2003).

Needless to say, in the realpolitik of everyday life, groups embold-ened by violence must generate victims in order to increase the glue between members, and are, therefore, insensitive to displays of victim-isation: community can be generated through the complicity of acts of perpetration, as they establish or reconfirm a clear boundary between "us" and "them" that strengthen identities and alliances. Examples abound. The period of the Rwandan genocide was one of extreme solidarity and collective pride among the Hutu genocidal killers; millions of thrilled Germans cheered Hitler's discourses that blamed Jews for the conditions of the treaty of Versailles that followed the defeat of Germany in the First World War and the economic crisis that followed; "hooliganism" is carried out with joy and collective energy by otherwise peaceful though socially marginalised men; "bullying" is done habitually by small groups of adolescents who establish "brotherhood" through their very acts; lynchings were carried out in the USA by otherwise law-abiding citizens involved in bizarre racist ceremonies under the banner of the Ku Klux Klan, and so on. Not infrequently, those perpetrators justify their behaviour on the basis of narratives of prior humiliation (or of potential future humiliation) in which the roles are reversed. They are taking revenge due to humiliations that they suffered in the immediate or remote past, familial or historic, documented or invented, or humiliation that they or their families or country would suffer if they do not carry on whatever they are doing.[15]

In the interpersonal arena, individually "hard-wired" traits such as a baseline level of arousal, in other words, the personal physiological proclivity toward reacting to novel situations with ease or with anxi-ety, play an important role. Anxious people tend to increase the level of anxiety in others, a trait (and effect) that enhances the probability of misunderstandings and escalations. In addition, anxious people (as well as people made anxious) have shown, in experimental situations, to be less able to discriminate whom to trust and whom not to (Con-way et al., 2008). This trait increases the probability of their victimising or being victimised in social exchanges. The same can be said of other personal variables, such as impulsivity, associated with an increased probability of enacting social performances that will be perceived by others as shaming or humiliating, and the capacity for empathy, the relative ability to place oneself in the other's position in a circumstance and experience their emotions. This trait has an important contribution in the process of engaging fluently in social interactions (see, e.g., Preston, Bechera, Grabowski, Damasio, & Damasio, 2007).

Given this multiplicity of intervening psychosocial and neurobiological variables interacting in everyday life, it may be clear by now that, as with any complex ("chaotic" in the sense provided by chaos theory) process, "pure" victims or "pure" perpetrators can be found only as outliers of a composite of multiple Gaussian curves.

While obvious, it is important to stress that whatever may be a shaming or humiliating experience for a given person might not be experienced as such for another, requiring caution on the part of the therapist so as not to attribute emotions to the patient just because the therapist would have experienced them in a similar situation, that is, by identification.

A colleague described to me an interesting experience. He was treating a rather successful young man of very humble origins, whose mother, burdened with children and worn out by a life of sacrifice, had offered him during his childhood, as he described it, scarce attention, contact, and tenderness. When the patient was six years old, a priest from a neighbouring parish invited the child to visit him, and established from then on a routine of frequent contacts—including sexual abuse—that lasted for the following six years. The priest was described by that man as a central figure in his life, an extremely tender and friendly presence, encouraging, and intellectually stimulating, a solid referent of reaffirmation that supported and protected the child throughout many vicissitudes during that period of his life. At the age of twelve, the child told the priest that he did not want to continue with their sexual activities, a request that the priest accepted without apparent resentment, while maintaining his mentoring and supportive role for a few years more, until he was moved to another parish. In the course of the treatment, the therapist explored at multiple points whether there were any feelings of resentment or rancour in the patient against the priest, as well as a "Stockholm syndrome"-like identification with the aggressor, but without any success. He finally convinced himself that the dominant feeling of the young man towards the priest was genuinely one of appreciation and affection for the tender support and clear guidance he received from that man during those crucial years of his life.

Returning to the main thrust of this presentation, let us examine the cast of characters that populate the scenario of situations that trigger experiences of shame and of humiliation.

The cast of characters

Narratives of social violence, including stories of shame and humiliation, include three central characters: *perpetrators, victims,* and *witnesses*. In its canonic structure, the perpetrator shames or humiliates the victim in front of the witness, who represents the "public eye" for the event. As mentioned above, however, there are many occasions when some of these characters may blend or fuse with one another or, in the specific case of perpetrators and witnesses, may have only a virtual presence. For instance, in plots in which the only inhabitants of the scene are the victimiser and the victim, one or the other may also occupy the role of witness. Such is the case of the torturers who, while torturing the victims, scorn them with contempt, labelling them as cowards or weaklings because they are screaming with pain, or of the rapist who adds to his violation the sardonic comment that the victim seems to be enjoying the rape (Sluzki, 1993). In many other scenarios, the witness inhabits the victim as an "inner voice" that comments, in a hostile testimony, a variation of "You should be ashamed!"

Quality and intensity of social emotions: intervening variables

Social situations that trigger shame or humiliation vary according to the traits of the participants and of the context.

Traits of the participants

The constructs "externalisation" and "internalisation" (an interpersonal process reflecting psychic defence mechanisms originally described by Freud as, respectively, projection and introjection (Freud, 1940e[1938]), and expanded by Klein in her discussion of projective and introjective identification (Klein, 1946)) are well known in the field of psychoanalysis. Their dominance in participants in everyday life as well as in extraordinary interactions will translate into disruptive, aggressive, destructive, and, broadly speaking, anti-social interventions, or in inhibited, insecure, anxious, and depressed behaviours, respectively (Achenbach, 1978; Eisenberg et al., 2001, among others). This predominance in the social arena will, in turn, result in narratives dominated by experiences of humiliation and/or shame in those involved.

In addition to these proclivities, individuals may also differ in terms of their capacity to anticipate or, on the contrary, become blindly entangled in situations that, due to their architecture and context, might generate reactions of shame or humiliation. In fact, the exact same situation and conditions may trigger one or the other emotion in different individuals. Those differences are frequently explained through what has been named the stress–diathesis hypothesis, a combination of early traumatic experiences and genetic predispositions or vulnerabilities. Scores of studies have demonstrated the important weight of genetic contributions to different dimensions relevant to the construct "temperament" (Buss & Plomin, 1984; Goldsmith, 2003; Plomin & Caspi, 1998). In turn, other research has shown that interactional traits of families of origin differ in children who lean towards experiencing social shame or humiliation—ultimately, internalisation or externalisation of the negative traits. These families have been located at either a chaotic spectrum or, at the other end of the spectrum, with a rigid style or extremely chaotic interactive modalities, with global attributions, emotional distance, humiliation as a mode of expressing disapproval, the use of expressions of love as reward and withdrawal of love as punishment, and severe physical or emotional punishment. These character traits, already apparent in childhood, have been shown to persist into adulthood (Caspi, Elder, & Bem, 1987; Dennissen, Asendorpf, & van Aken, 2008).

In sum, modulated by genetic proclivities and a variety of life experiences, we carry within us a choir of internalised "witnesses", contributing substantively to what we vaguely experience in our adult moral consciousness. They are a cacophony of internalised voices that include those of our parents, family members, friends, teachers, trusted confessors, leaders who judge our actions with commentaries, and guides. Sometimes they are gentle and tender, sometimes permissive and indulgent, sometimes severe or even sadistic and debasing, in keeping with the broad mandates of our culture, actual external voices, and the varied architecture of our current daily or exceptional life experiences.

The processes that orientate a given experience towards shame or humiliation, as well as the intensity of the experience, are sensitive to the effect of many variables, some discussed above, some to be summarily described below. They include personal style (genetic and epigenetic traits), the actual behaviours displayed by or attributed to each of the characters (including witnesses perceived as hostile or friendly), the repetitive or unusual nature of the event, the degree of proportionality between acts and reaction by all the participants, the presence or absence of a context of crisis, whether a victimisation (if there is victimisation) is isolated or collective, and the degree of risk entailed in redress (Figure 4.2).

Hostile and friendly witnesses

To start with, let us portray a trivial social situation: you are leaving a supermarket carrying a paper bag filled to the brim with groceries of every kind. Suddenly, you trip on a bump in the pavement, stumble, and fall ignominiously. The contents of your bag—a variety of fruits and vegetables, a small carton of milk, toilet paper, cereal boxes—fly in all directions. Quickly glancing around, you realise that nobody witnessed the accident. The situation then becomes one of those events that you want to undo, that is, to edit out of the record of your life as quickly as possible: you pick yourself up in a rush, collect all your groceries, rearrange your clothes if in disarray and brush off if slightly soiled, and continue walking at a reasonable speed, perhaps only looking back with annoyance at the bump in the sidewalk

Add "intensity" points for	Subtract "intensity" points for
High reactivity of subject	Low reactivity of subject
Hostile witness	Friendly witness
Focus on imminent trait	Focus on ephemeral traits
Disproportion act/scorn	High proportion act/scorn
No prior crisis	Context of crisis
Hopelessness among victims	Solidarity among victims
High risk for redress	Low risk for redress

Figure 4.2.   Intervening variables in intensity of emotion.

that attacked your dignity, and relieved that nobody witnessed the event.

Let us add a character to the story. A person that was standing nearby saw what happened to you, and rushes to help you as you get up, asking you with some alarm in their voice whether you are hurt, expressing relief when you reassure them, and commenting that a similar situation happened to them a few days before precisely in that very spot, adding some complaints about the bad condition of the pavement or of the world in general. We have in front of us a paradigmatic *friendly witness*: their slightly exaggerated expression of concern and offer to help is on all accounts in solidarity. Further, their comment that a similar accident happened to them takes away any assumption that it was your fault, while their complaint about the condition of the pavement or of the world offers an externalising option, proposing that the pavement or the world are to be blamed for your misstep, not you. Through all those displays, that solicitous friendly witness will reduce the intensity of the negative emotion— shame, in all likelihood—that may accompany that experience. In fact, in the long run you may find his excessive solicitousness annoying, as it ends up magnifying an event that you wish to minimise.

Let us now imagine the very same scene, the only difference being that the person who observed your mishap, instead of running to help, begins to laugh, insensitive not only to your potential physical pain, but also to your potentially wounded self-esteem. This witness's laughter defines the situation as a display of sloppiness or lack of care or skill on your part, not very different from what we see in a television sit-com, where we might find the pathetic physical awkwardness displayed by the actors as funny, mainly thanks to the clues provided by the (generally pre-recorded) soundtrack of a giggling audience. You are in front of a *hostile witness*—offering you a target for externalising your critic. In those circumstances, you will be tempted to confront that witness, perhaps while still on the floor, with a hostile comment of your own ("What are you laughing at, you idiot!") in order to neutralise your *humiliation* by balancing the interaction. Or, if you sense that the laughing witness is somehow deranged or potentially threatening, you might give him a contemptuous glance and, picking yourself and your belongings up, exit the scene with as much of a dignified pace as you can muster, while ruminating over some nasty comment or a fantasy of revenge until you calm down and, in the long run, forget the event. That witness has intensified the probability as well as the intensity of an experience of *humiliation*, perhaps tinted with a touch of *shame* if you did not dare confront a witness who transformed a minor mishap into a (minor) affront.

Regardless of the presence or absence of witnesses, if stumbling and falling has also triggered an accidental loss of sphincter control, that is, if you peed on yourself, or if the fall led to an awkward display of undergarments, the social experience of *shame* will take over, and you will aim to escape the scene as quickly as possible, avoiding even the most friendly of witnesses.

Needless to say, if you belong to the class of those who internalise and feel easily ashamed, a person labelled as timid or insecure, in all likelihood you will experience shame even if the witness is extremely friendly. If, instead, you are prone to externalisation (you might have been labelled by somebody as aggressive, paranoid, or perhaps even sociopathic), you will feel humiliated by the event ("Damn pavement made me fall!" "I'll sue the store for this!") and might even mistreat the Good Samaritan who tried to help you, as if he had somehow contributed to the event taking place.

Finally, it could happen that the witness behaves neither solicitously nor contemptuously but with *indifference*, looking at you as if the mishap did not involve him at all. This display of social indifference, rather uncommon and negatively viewed in our society,[16] might lead you, if you are prone to shame, to be grateful to your fate for a witness who behaves as if you were invisible. If you are prone to humiliation, you might label that indifference as a hostile behaviour, meriting a position as the target of your anger ("What are you looking at? Never seen somebody falling?"). In sum, as already stated above, in practice there is seldom such a role as a purely "neutral witness", except when explicitly sanctioned as such, for example, a couples therapist, or a professional mediator (even though in most cases each party will present evidence of a reality that invites that mediating witness to take his side).

To add complexity to the role, there are three-party scenes in which the witnesses add insult to injury by actively siding with actual external perpetrators and therefore legitimising their acts. One example among many would be a parent who looks severely at a child while the child is being punished by the other parent for a minor or major infraction (in contrast to, for instance, a scene in which one denigrates and the other subsequently takes the offspring to the side to calm him tenderly, either disqualifying *de facto* the other's comments or at least defining the offspring as not deserving denigration, thus reducing the emotional impact of the whole experience).[17] In sum, as is shown in Figure 4.2, a hostile witness acts as co-perpetrator, increasing the intensity of the experience, while a friendly witness tends to moderate it.

Immanent and ephemeral traits as focus

Allusions to an individual's immanent (inherent, intrinsic) traits tend to generate more intensity in an experience of shame or humiliation than allusions to more ephemeral traits. Therefore, regardless of the circumstances that may have triggered it, the impact of a comment such as "You are incompetent!" (or "stupid", or "mean", or "mad", in any of its multiple versions) hits an individual harder than "You are looking sleepy", or "behaving distractedly", or "feeling mean today". This difference between the lapidary "being" and the circumstantial "behaving", further temporalised by the "today", contains the difference between the hopelessness of a fixed trait and the hope for change of an ephemeral one.[18] In fact, this distinction is discussed frequently as a recommendation in books about child rearing, where authors stress the importance of using circumstantial attributions when referring to negative traits and immanent attributions in regard to positive traits.[19]

Contexts of crisis as modulator

In contexts of collective crisis, such as, for instance, a fire in our building, an evacuation because of an earthquake, or because our neighbourhood is being targeted by a raid, many behaviours of others that otherwise would be experienced by us as humiliating or shaming become acceptable. The person in charge of an evacuation may, for instance, shout at and even insult a person who is remiss in reacting or in following her instructions without the other taking it as a personal affront. Further, if the recipient of those injunctions does not accommodate them, it can be predicted that the otherwise uninvolved witnesses will divide among those who join the leader in haranguing the misbehaving person and those who will approach her and cajole her in a friendly fashion to move along. "Good cop/bad cop" occurs spontaneously not only in fiction, but in many real-life scenarios.

Characteristics of the mandates of the dominant culture

The public, as well as the internalised eye, incorporates and reconstitutes the mandates of the surrounding community: family, group of friends, clan, neighbourhood, institution, and broader society. It informs and reminds us of what is considered appropriate and what inappropriate, what is good and what is evil, what is noble and what vile.

Cultures that support a highly hierarchical and oppressive social order, parroted by the government-controlled media, with praise for honour-based arguments and a rhetoric where the polarities of valour–cowardice (traits defined respectively as honourable and dishonourable), triumph–defeat (commended and unacceptable), due obedience–dissension (respectful and disrespectful), us–them (the chosen, superior, privileged, pure, and the inferior, despicable, subhuman) will increase the frequency and intensity of negative social emotions. These, as well as added elements such as a code of honour tied to "blood debts", facilitate experiences of *humiliation* as well as its mandate of revenge to repair the honour.

A failure in fulfilling that mandate is tied in turn to shame, pulling the subject towards hiding or escaping, in some cultures offering self-immolation as an honourable way of escaping or appeasing the other's critical eye. Such is the case of the Japanese pre-modern culture of the Samurai, where the polarity honour–shame had a central role in the construction of their collective and personal identity. That trait is still pervasive today in Japan (Ikegami, 2003), where public errors or failure also require public ritualised apologies, filled with expressions of shame, to repair the damage.

Those cultural mandates clash with the rising (mainly Western) preoccupation with, and defence of, human rights, where experiences of shame as well as humiliation call for the restoration of the victim's dignity through fair judgement of the perpetrators, and/or empathic dialogue, sincere apologies, and, if possible, reconciliation. This ideology is transparent in practices of mediation, understood not as a negotiation of agreements through give-and-take, but as the facilitation of transformed narratives that establish a consensual basis for understanding and resolving conflictive events (Cobb, 2004).

In this regard, it bears repeating that the ideological basis for the doctrine of human rights was established less than 200 years ago, and its consensus among Anglo-European countries has increased only during the past sixty years, embodied in the United Nations' 1948 Universal Declaration of Human Rights and its subsequent expansions. We are witnessing a process by which what was "the natural order" of many oppressive and discretionary practices is becoming acts against individual rights.[20] Paradoxically, this ideological shift does not reduce the individual experience of humiliation but increases it, as many acts that were considered normal mechanisms for the maintenance of social order (such as discrimination against minorities "so they keep their place", wife-beating "if they are disrespectful", mistreatment of children "so they learn", and of the elderly "so they don't bother others") became, under this new lens, unacceptable wounds to their personal dignity and collective rights.

The head of a family of Moroccan origin living in Belgium for the past twelve years was utterly surprised and distressed when his adolescent elder son, who appeared black and blue at the public school he was attending after a disciplinary beating he received from his father, was interviewed by the representatives of a social welfare agency and sent to a centre for abused children. His family was informed that, if they wanted their son back at home in the near future, they would have to follow a family therapy treatment as well as several other stipulations. The father, both humiliated and offended while doing his best to accommodate the judge's expectations, exclaimed, "That is the way I was educated! How do you expect hm to obey me otherwise!", a perfect example of a cross-cultural conflict based on norms that are socially acceptable in one culture and unacceptable in another (for a detailed discussion of this case, see Sluzki, 2004).

Humiliating experiences as heroic deeds

Some circumstances have the potential for generating humiliation, but are tolerated and even exalted when perceived by the recipient and by third parties as enacted for the common good. They are, in fact, the mirror image of what has been labelled above as "shame for abdication of the self". We can continue with a vignette used as an example in this category.

A Year 2 child has thrown a piece of chalk at the classroom blackboard while the teacher was writing on it. The teacher declares angrily that such behaviour is unacceptable and asks who has done it. Nobody answers. She then tells the students that she will punish the whole class unless the culprit comes forward. After a period of silence, another child, not the one who threw the chalk, gets up and tells her that he has done it. He is brought to a corner at the front of the classroom and asked to sit on a tall chair while the teacher places a dunce's cap on his head.[21] The noble action, perhaps only known as such by the real culprit and the victim, neutralises the experience of humiliation.

The eldest of three sisters had accepted in silence the repeated sexual abuse by her father since early childhood. He had convinced her that, if she let him continue with the abuse without resistance, he would not "have to" molest her younger sisters. While enjoying the privilege, she was profoundly repelled by the experience of abuse, but continued to accept his predatory behaviour, thinking each time that she was protecting her younger sisters. The revelation, years later, that in spite of what she considered her sacrifice, her father had secretly also been abusing one of her sisters led the two sisters to denounce the father to legal authorities. The older sister sensed that her years of shame and sacrifice had been for naught. The younger sister, in turn, with the knowledge that her older sister had also been abused, felt relief, no longer alone in carrying the secret. (While it is possible to assume that the older sister's decision to denounce the father was also out of anger at his having betrayed her by robbing her of her assumption of a position of privilege in the family, the revelation takes away from her any assumption of heroism for her role, pushing her from a tolerated shame into acting out of humiliation.)

Direction of the process of change in the therapeutic context[22]

In order to propose a therapeutic course for patients who appear to be trapped in a world view tinted by one of the two negative emotions discussed above, I shall resort to the "terrible simplification" of reducing the set of variables into a binary matrix (see Matrix 1).

The set of matrices that follows establishes the schematic interaction between two key variables, which are the personal style of the individual and the nature of the witness. The two variables selected interact, as mentioned above, with other variables that sometimes have greater and sometimes lesser weight, such as the nature and context of the scene (did the event, if a single event happens to be the focus, take place in the intimacy of the home, in the street, at a bar, or in a prison cell?), how proportionate are the actions and reactions of perpetrator, victim, and witness, and the relative toxicity of perpetrator and witness.[23] (While these two variables are central in our discussion, the same approach could be used to specify the varied impact of either of the other two variables we have discussed.)

The point of departure of the process is an unspecified, potentially traumatic or destabilising event that has a possible negative reading by the protagonists or third parties: stumbling on the pavement, a circumstantial comment at an otherwise innocuous social interaction, a rape while jogging across a park in the evening, the malignant comments of a torturer during a session of torture, a marital infidelity— that is, a broad variety of possible scenarios that might contain minimal, substantial, and severe traumatic potential. Each of them *may* generate an experience of shame or humiliation in the subject who describes himself as a victim of the other or of the circumstances (regardless of the agreement or disagreement between the different participants in terms of their respective locus as perpetrators, victims, and witness).

Figure 4.3 reflects the notion that the intensity of the situation's impact—whichever it may be—is mitigated by the presence and actions of an empathic witness, while it is exacerbated by the presence and actions of a hostile one. A hostile witness, including the witnessing enactment of a perpetrator, increases not only the intensity of the experience, but potentiates the possibility of its lingering, long-term effect.

The next two figures specify alternative trajectories of the *therapeutic process*, taking as their point of departure patients who present a complaint during a consultation that directly or indirectly shows the dominance of shame or humiliation as a result of an event that continues to haunt them. Both matrices reflex the assumption that therapists,

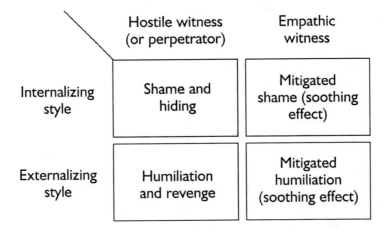

Figure 4.3.   Matrix showing the effects of the presence of a hostile witness and that of an empathic one on a situation that causes shame or humiliation.

in addition to being experts in the facilitation of change processes, become empathic witnesses of the patients' narratives through gently listening, echoing, resonating, commenting, remembering, completing, modifying, and reframing their stories with them. However, they might also be relevant to those circumstances in which an occasional empathic witness accomplishes an "on-the-spot" therapeutic function.

Figure 4.4 assumes that the dominant emotional experience anchoring the story described by the patient is one of *shame*. It might

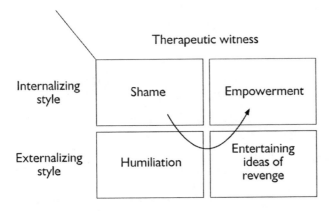

Figure 4.4.   Matrix depicting the effect of a therapeutic witness on a situation where the emotional experience is one of shame.

appear as a description of repetitive, flooding experiences of shame, or as the thematic reiteration of an episode that is defined as the point of departure for symptoms or conflicts where shame may be inferred.

Figure 4.5 depicts one direction of the therapeutic process, specifically, a progressive transformation of the traumatic history towards one that will elicit humiliation. The transformation facilitates a mutation in the structure of the story, externalising the source of the assault or causing dissonance between the self- and other-image and the self- and other-attribution. This process might even include the facilitation and legitimisation of ideas of revenge (concordant with the "new" experience of humiliation), freeing the patient from the self-defeating experience of remembering and shaming as the story is transformed into one in which the patient acquires "voice", power, and autonomy.

I should add that I do not believe a narrative that generates humiliation is in any way "better" than one that generates shame. I do believe, however, that patients stuck in one story are stuck in its emotional correlates, while events and contexts contain multiple possible stories. Therefore, destabilising the story tied to the original emotion and facilitating its transformation frees them from that emotional trap and allows them to evolve towards narratives that do not anchor symptoms, helping them to become more competent in a complex, multi-layered world.

A thirty-year-old woman, executive secretary in a non-governmental organisation, was referred to me by another patient who

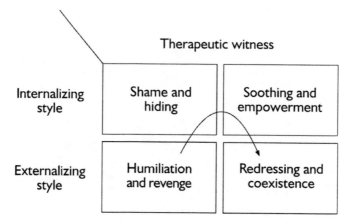

Figure 4.5. Matrix showing the orientation of the therapeutic process with narratives anchored in humiliation.

shares offices with her. My patient had had a conversation with the woman in which she told her, in tears, that a couple of weeks before, she was crossing a park in the evening on her way home, and was attacked by an assailant, dragged behind some trees, and raped. While she did report the attack to the police—who interviewed her exhaustively—and was examined at a hospital emergency room, the only other person who knew about the event was her live-in boyfriend. He did not want to talk about her assault any more and did not want her to talk to anybody else about it.

During the first consultation, this petite, thin woman sat in a corner of her armchair, establishing little eye contact, talking in a low, inhibited voice about the reason for the consultation. Her body language, gestures, voice inflection, and tone conveyed both sadness and shame. I began to explore the violent attack of which she had been the victim, avoiding scopophilic questions, focusing initially more on the scenario and then on the plot. The assault took place in the early evening in a park that she crossed frequently to reach her house. She added that she should have paid attention to the newspaper coverage of a rapist predator that had attacked in that neighbourhood twice. She said she could have taken the longer road and walked around, rather than through, the park. After a long day at work, she took the underground to a station near her house, as usual. Her live-in boyfriend, who frequently picked her up there by car, called her at the last minute to inform her that he would not make it in time. So she did as she usually did, walked home across the park, where she was attacked. The attacker surprised her, caught her from behind by the neck, lifted her off her feet (she described him as strong and tall while she was, as I mentioned, small and thin), and told her that he would kill her if she screamed or defended herself. He dragged her behind some thick bushes, disrobed her partially, and raped her. Afterwards, the rapist threatened that if she went to the police, he would find her and kill her. As she heard him leaving, she composed her clothing and, crying, ran to her house. Her boyfriend immediately called the police, who instructed them that she should go to the emergency room of a nearby hospital. There she received emergency care and instructions for follow-up preventative care, and met with the police to provide the necessary information. I then explored possible "toxic" commentaries offered by those with whom she had interacted since the incident: the rapist told her that she was dressed provocatively—implying that she provoked the rape—as well as saying "you asked for it by crossing the park in the dark". As she arrived home, crying, she told her boyfriend what had happened. His first distressed comments were, "Why did you cross the park instead of walking around it?" and "But why didn't you defend yourself?", but then he was supportive and co-operative. However, he later told her that it would be better if she did not mention the event to anybody, family or friends (including female friends, many of whom were wives of his friends), "because then everybody would know about it". However, both police officers and the emergency room personnel were described as careful, respectful, and professional.

During the first and second interviews, the type and style of questions I posed began to pick apart a story that was filled with self-blaming nuances, anchored in part in her own prejudices and in part on the comments made by the rapist and her boyfriend. Questions I asked during my exploration included, for instance, "You described the assailant as tall and strong, and that he was holding you from behind with his arms around your neck, and yourself sort of hanging there in the air, scared beyond belief and fearing for your life. Am I correct? Did I understand your description clearly? Now, given that scenario, how do you think you could have defended yourself?" "How do you believe your sister and your female friends would react if you told them what happened to you? What would they think and feel? Would they react with indifference, rejection, or solidarity?" "What is your theory about why your boyfriend didn't want you to mention this ordeal to anybody?" "What would be the effect on yourself if you couldn't share the story of this attack that you have been the victim of with any of the women within your intimate circle, your sister, your friends?" "Before this terrible incident, what was your opinion of women who said they had been raped? Was there any change in your view on the matter?" "What is your opinion about the comment that creep made about your clothing?" "In your view, were you dressed differently on this occasion than on others?" "What do you think your boyfriend felt when you entered the house crying, desperately telling him about the rape, in the light of his not having picked you up at the underground station?" "In your view, would there be any relation between those feelings and his request that you not tell anybody?" etc.

The progressive deconstruction of the original story, seeded with self-blame and shame, and the construction of one in which she was the innocent victim of a malignant act resulted in a noticeable change in both her non-verbal behaviour—she sat in a more relaxed and comfortable position, with good visual contact and using a firmer voice—as well as in the content of her conversation. Angry and contemptuous comments about the rapist started to emerge, as well as an increasingly agentic stance, including her decision to talk about it with her sister and her female friends, defying her boyfriend, "who will have to accept it, like it or not". She appeared more critical of her boyfriend, whom she said she felt supported by in some aspects but not in others. She mentioned a couple of subsequent confrontations with him, accusing him of blaming her for the rape. There were some escalations that placed the relationship at risk but that seemed to be lessened when he confessed to her his guilty feelings for not having taken good care of her, as he also had read in the newspaper about the rapist in the area but ended up not picking her up at the station for a trivial reason. He apologised, an act that she experienced as genuine, and that led to a rapprochement . . . and to their first sexual encounter since the date of the rape, an intimacy that she sensed as "cleaning her inside".

During the next two interviews, the dominant emotion was rage because of the humiliation. She explored revenge fantasies against the rapist, which she then toned down "as she was a pacifist", to locking him up and "throwing the key in the river". Fortunately, part of her wish was accomplished a few weeks later, when the predator was identified by one of his other victims (not by this woman, as she never saw his face), arrested, and indicted. Our patient was ready to "help throw the key in the river" by testifying during the trial, since his semen matched samples obtained during her visit to the emergency room. To her relief, she could also confirm that he was HIV negative, a concern that had been upsetting her until then.

I saw her for a total of five sessions, the first two in consecutive weeks, and then every two weeks. During the last one, she expressed her appreciation for the conversations we had had, which she said helped her very much. In turn, I defined myself mainly as a witness to her many resources, and praised her lucidity and courage throughout the difficult process of regaining faith in the world and in herself.

I learnt indirectly that she presented her testimony during the rapist's trial, and that he was sentenced to prison for several decades. She ended up leaving her boyfriend, is involved in a new relationship, and continues her professional activities with energy and good humour, as before.

It should be noted that the direct transformation of the story of an event that elicits shame into one that allows the recovery of self-esteem *without* going through an intermediate story of humiliation—and its unavoidable notions of redress or revenge—is seldom feasible. It is usually experienced as a trivial exhortation along the lines of "Don't feel the way you do!" but does not modify the relationship between the self and the other or favour an ethical balance between self- and other-responsibility. The same can be said of attempts at deconstructing and changing stories that had evoked the experience of humiliation without introducing shame components in the process of transforming the stories, as otherwise we will simply muffle but keep alive paralysing ruminations of revenge. This will serve as a prelude for the next proposal.

The matrix depicted in Figure 4.5 explores an alternative scenario, one in which the dominant persistent emotion evoked by a given narrative is humiliation. The orientation proposed for the therapeutic process is to facilitate a progressive transformation of the story towards one that would elicit shame, that is, favouring an internalisa-tion of the critical voice and even the emergence of fantasies of escap-ing or hiding—consonant with the "new" experience of shame—to then freeing the patient from the trap of the narrative of humiliation towards one of reparation and, perhaps ultimately, of coexistence.

Victims of extreme violence are able to free themselves from the one-note trap of revenge when their story is enriched as we recover or evoke the experience of shame. At times, this later emotion is, as we mentioned above, inoculated by the perpetrator or by hostile witnesses, sometimes by accusing themselves of having "lost their own dignity" through pleas or cries (or denunciations of innocents, under torture). The passage through shame does not imply leaving the victims trapped in self-blame. It is, however, necessary sometimes as an intermediary station towards forgiving themselves and recovering their own dignity.

Juan, a twenty-seven-year-old Latin American male, says in a flat voice at the outset of his first consultation that he is here following the exhortations of his family, who was fed up with his ill temper and verbal violence. He explains that what he calls "his family" are really an uncle and his family, with whom he has been living for almost ten years, since he left his country. He acknowledges that he has a very "short fuse", but he is constantly angry with them because they do not want to support him emotionally or economically in his plans to return to his country to take revenge for what was done to him.

He then proceeded to explain that, while still an adolescent, he became one more of the legion of "desaparecidos" in Argentina, his country of origin. He had been kidnapped from his home by an armed group from the police or the military in power, blindfolded, and transported to a secret detention centre. There he was tortured mercilessly for several weeks to obtain information that he did not have about secret plans associated with names of people he did not know. It was a daily nightmare, he stated, and he had lost all hope of surviving. However, one day, still blindfolded and handcuffed, he had been transported by car to a desolate area and dumped out. He was convinced that he would be shot to death there and then. But, when he heard the car leaving, he managed to free himself from the handcuffs and blindfold and found himself alone, half-naked, in an open pasture in the countryside: the torturers, to his surprise, had set him free. He walked to a road that he saw in the distance and, after signalling for passing cars to stop, he was transported by a charitable soul to a nearby small town. There, he was able to phone his parents, who, enormously relieved, rushed by car to pick him up. A few days later, he was sent by his parents to the USA to live with his uncle to escape the risk of a repeat of that nightmarish experience in a society where the impunity of the government and its violence was becoming the rule. Since then he had been living with his uncle and his family in the USA.

He keeps on wondering obsessively why they pinpointed and kidnapped him. He mused, unconvinced, that perhaps a friend mentioned his name under torture, or a hypothetical resentful neighbour denounced him. He denies having had any kind of political commitment, and he assumes that they finally let him go because he convinced them of that, in addition to the sheer luck of his not having died under torture.

As time passed in his country of exile, he began and dropped out of college courses twice, and he started and abandoned a variety of jobs. On each occasion he describes being obsessed by endless rumination on plans for revenge, fantasising day and night about returning to his country to find and kill his torturers. He had difficulty sleeping, his mind occupied with designing different schemes and methods to carry out these plans. His malaise and irritation increased day by day, and he was furious with his family, who not only did not support his ideation, but also was becoming less tolerant of his obsessive themes and his lack of contact with present reality. Over the past few years, he had had a couple of girlfriends, but those relationships followed the same pattern: these young women were initially moved by his suffering, making efforts at soothing him and nourishing him, but ended up exhausted by his monothematic obsessions.

During the subsequent interviews, in addition to stories about his childhood and his family and his current relations, this patient described in detail the scenarios related to his capture, his liberation, and his subsequently leaving his country. His overall attitude was a mixture of indifference and arrogance, with frequent contemptuous comments about his current family's lack of empathy, as well as rather grandiose ideas of what he would do if/when he returned to his country of origin, including fantasies of organising and co-ordinating a commando-like group that would locate and kill those involved in the official torture apparatus: "If Wiesenthal, the Nazi hunter, could do it, why can't I?" Notably, his experiences while he was "disappeared", that is, what happened to him while he was at the torture centre, were conspicuously absent. The stories that the patient shared with me had a "disappeared" area whose boundaries I carefully respected, assuming that he would open the doors of that hell for me in due time.

That moment arrived in a session in which he told me of a dream that startled him: he found himself stark naked in the middle of a road full of cars going in both directions. When I asked him what emotion accompanied his dream, he answered, "I was terribly ashamed." I asked, "Ashamed of what and in front of whom?" and he answered, "Of being naked with all those people in the cars who were looking at me." He was about to try to change the subject, but I asked him to remain silent for a while, and to connect with the emotion that had been triggered by the dream. We remained in silence perhaps for half a minute, and tears starting rolling down his cheeks. At that moment, I felt anxious and moved, and had to fight my own temptation to swiftly switch subjects. Instead, I said to him, in a tender voice, "The shame." He covered his face with his hands and started to cry uncontrollably. I kept silent for a while, and then he said, still sobbing, "You must be thinking I am crazy, crying like a baby over a dream like that." I answered, "Well, you were swallowed by a nightmare from which it is difficult to wake up."[24] To which he answered, "But can you imagine being stark naked and tied to a metal bed while they torture you with cattle prods and, in addition, they are also laughing at you?" And in that way, from one moment to the next, he introduced me as a witness to a brutal scenario in that torture centre where, naked and tied to a metal frame, he was being tortured with electric charges while the torturers were laughing at him, the sadistic opposite of empathy. "And I would scream and they would laugh, I would pee and shit on myself and they would laugh, I would tell them that I would sign any kind of confession that they wanted, and they would laugh and continue with the prods. And what makes me more furious with myself is that afterwards, rolling on the floor of that room, I did what they wanted all over again, because I cried, pleaded, begged them, invented a confession, I don't know what. But that wouldn't stop them, it would happen again and, I don't know, they were well trained and knew very well what they were doing. And there I would be, crying again, begging again, confessing I don't know what, and they were there, laughing at me. Once I asked them "What are you laughing at?" and they answered with contempt, "At you being a sissy, a cry-baby, at your shouting and confessing to anything."

A bridge had been crossed. During the following sessions, he went on to detail all his "confessions", inventions that he made up to try to placate them and to stop the torture. He would describe himself as innocent or, at most, a naïve patsy of others, who tricked him into becoming involved in minor illegal activities, giving them the names of friends, neighbours, high school professors, whomever he could think of, while the torturers laughed at him, telling him that he was a lousy liar and that they didn't believe one word of what he was saying, but that they would yank the truth from him, while he was swearing in terror that it was all true. This scenario was described accompanied by expressions of unbearable shame as well as guilt for having potentially implicated so many totally innocent people with his pseudo-confessions. "Everybody [all those being tortured] did it," he would argue. "I could hear many others being tortured, and everybody confessed to anything, everybody invented stories to try to stop the torture." But that argument did not reduce his experience of guilt and shame. I asked him, "If you could have been a fly on the wall looking at yourself in that situation, naked, tied, tortured, what opinion would you have had about that person?" "Well," he answered, "I would have felt sorry for that poor guy." After a moment of silence, I repeated, "You would have felt sorry for him." Once again, a change of tone and of mood followed, as he started to cry, this time without self-deprecating comments, with some tenderness. Disassociated, he seemed to be looking at himself in that situation, saying repeatedly, while sobbing, "Poor guy! Poor guy!"

When that specific session ended he did something he had not done before: he hugged me when saying goodbye. From that point, the emotional climate of the therapy changed, becoming more intimate, calmer, more involved in what he ended up calling "sweeping and cleaning", a critical examining of each of his self-deprecations (mainly derived from the torturers' cruel comments, which had remained engraved in his mind, torturing and debasing him again on a daily basis). Concurrently, his obsessional themes of revenge against the torturers diminished, as the experiences of torture kept alive in the theatre of his memory seemed to reduce in intensity and frequency. He also began to express compassion for his local family, "poor, kind people whom I have been torturing all these years". Shortly thereafter he told me that he had apologised to them and begun to rebuild their relationship, while expressing more comfort with his current job. "If I catch one of those torturers, I swear to you that I'll kill him . . . but I am not going to give them my life," was one of the assertions that may summarise his transformation.

This treatment—one or two sessions per week—lasted six months. Two years later, I had a circumstantial encounter with Juan, who told me that he was reasonably happy with life. He was studying again while working full-time, living on his own but in close contact with his uncle and family, and had a group of friends, which he did not have when I saw him, as well as a girlfriend. Occasionally he still has dreams of being tortured and he "wakes up with relief and the joy of living in freedom". For his next vacation he was also planning, with some trepidation, to return to his country—where the military dictatorship had been replaced by a democratic government—to visit family but also to try to explore whether any of those whom he had mentioned under torture had been victimised as a result of his "confessions", or whether the lies he had concocted had been taken as what they were, inventions that were a product of his despair.

A view that discriminates between experiences of shame and experiences of humiliation adds clarity to the dynamics of those processes both at the intra- and the interpersonal level. It also helps explain the tenacity of the narratives that contain those intense emotions and, as has been detailed above, it provides an outline that may guide us throughout the therapeutic process

Once revealed, the traumatic narratives that trap the subjects (individuals, groups, institutions, or nations) in the pain of negative emotions as well as their correlation of social withdrawal, self-deprecation, and inaction in the case of shame, and bitter ruminations or enactments of revenge in the case of humiliation, open the door to enriching therapeutic alternatives. Those narratives can be transformed into ones that include responsibility, authorship, and change. The therapeutic process requires, none the less, time and skill, given (i) the systemic coherence of any narrative, even more so when tied to particularly painful experiences or to persistent symptoms, (ii) the social advantage that some of them entail, and (iii) the social pressure that the milieu, frequently captured by those stories, may exert toward their retention.

The therapeutic guidelines proposed in this chapter will help facilitate not only the deconstruction of stories of shame or of humiliation, but also their transformation into a resolution that frees them from the trap of pain while revealing an ethical and freer world for them, and for us all.

Notes

1. This story of the composer whose jacket self-destructs is one of a set of stories (connected, in fact, only through the tailcoat) of the film *Tales of Manhattan*, directed by Julien Duvivier after his arrival in the US in 1942, after escaping the German occupation of France. The six episodes of this film were written by a team of first-class writers, several of them also escapees from Nazism (and later black-listed during McCarthy's witch hunt): Alan Campbell, Ben Hecht, Samuel Hoffenstein, FerencMolnár, and Donald Ogden Stewart. The main actors in this episode were a young Charles Laughton as the composer, and Elsa Lancaster, his wife in real life, as his wife.

2. A sovereign might, for political reasons, or even due to ethical sensitivity or to the wish to redress prior acts of oppression, behave with his

subjects as if he were "one of them", as a peer. Those actions might increase his popularity because it could be seen by the populus as a choice, and, therefore, as a noble or democratic gesture. However, it might also be understood as an expression of weakness and, therefore, be viewed with contempt. These considerations apply to any relationship between people of uneven power.

3. This description echoes "labelling theory" or "theory of social reactivity" that, taking as a point of departure the notion of the social construction of the self (Mead, 1982), describes the impact that the categorisations or descriptions made by the Other has on the individual's identity, in a sort of self-fulfilling prophecy of both positive and negative descriptors (Scheff, 1999).

4. The list of thematic categories, as well as these assertions, follows the guidelines and results of research conducted by Baumeister, Stillwell, and Wotman (1990) on autobiographic narratives of violent interpersonal conflicts in which the informants defined themselves as perpetrators or as victims. The main difference these researchers found between both positions is that, as perpetrator, people tended to define their behaviours as contextually reasonable, while stories where they were victims tended to define the aggression by the other as arbitrary, gratuitous, and incomprehensible. A yet unpublished replication of this study that I conducted on 300 subjects (this time focused on recalled stories of victimisation in both positions) confirms these observations, and the observations detailed in the next paragraph.

5. "The memory wars are enacted by critical efforts within societies that allow their stories to emerge in the public debate" (Lara, 2007, p. 137). Political and ethical evolution takes place only in societies where this debate is allowed.

6. One side of those views, both the idealised view of the past and the nobility of their (Southern) cause *vs.* the arrogance and destructiveness of the North, can be found rather transparently in Margaret Mitchell's classic 1936 novel, *Gone with the Wind*, as well as in its remarkably faithful film version.

7. You, reader, are also a witness for me. Think of my comment about that photograph of the Vietnamese girl. I included it in the text because it came to mind as an association while writing the previous sentence. But, how much of this association was propelled by my wish to have an image of your image of me as a compassionate, sensitive person? And how much was aimed at disassociating, in (my view of) your view of me, your image of me from that of the imperial foreign policies of the country where I have been living for the past forty years? Ultimately, is writing a

book, or an article, purely for purposes of transmission of knowledge and stimulation of ideas, or it is in part because of my wish to enhance your (I hope positive) view of me as a result of your reading this? The spiral of reciprocal perspectives twirls *ad infinitum*.

8. I wish to acknowledge my personal recognition of Suzanne Retzinger and Thomas Scheff (e.g., Scheff & Retzinger 1991a,b, 2000), who have made important contributions to the theme in its many dimensions and whose work, presentations, and extremely cherished friendship have stimulated my own explorations on the topic. This list of valuable contributors should also include the indefatigable Evelyn Lindner (cf. 2001, 2006) as well as Miller (1993), and Harper and Hoopes (1990.)

9. This "other" can be virtual, as in the case of an omniscient God that may be experienced as a severe or kind witness to sins of the faithful.

10. A statistically significant proportion of battered woman describe having been raised in a milieu that resorts to shame as a dominant disciplinary style (Buchbinder & Eisikovitz, 2003, among others.) It should be noted that these findings have been the object of a valuable feminist critique, arguing that it reduces the responsibility of the perpetrators, as it risks being used to blame the battered woman for her own victimisation, thus negating the socio-cultural roots of violence against women. However, the solid evidence that associates battering victimisation of women by their mates and childhood experiences of having been witnesses of victims of violence and shaming behaviours cannot be disregarded, and neither does it reduce at all the responsibility of the perpetrators. A description that is both feminist and systemic may argue that those early experiences help to explain the low capacity of those women for self-assertion, their weak "voice", their learnt helplessness and lower social competency. But it is the experiences of abusive relationships later in life and a culture that condones those practices that intertwines with the former, closing off alternatives.

11. Shame, and acts aimed at avoiding it or neutralising its effect, are one of the central motors of social processes in Japanese society. Correspondingly, in that culture, expressions of shame and of self-depre-cation are core components of the request for forgiveness (Lazare, 2004).

12. The word *humiliation* shares its etymological root with one of the cardi-nal virtues, namely, *humility*, characterised by generous, respectful, and modest behaviour. Its opposite is the vainglory (i.e., vaneidouse glory, or boasting) of *pride*, a trait that, together with anger, greed, sloth, lust, envy, and gluttony, completes the list of what the Christian canon defines as the seven deadly sins, the root of all other sins.

13. The savagery displayed by the Serbs during their invasion of those neigh-
    bouring countries with an Islamic majority, such as Bosnia-Herzegovina
    and Kosovo, was in turn the fruit of the invasion of those territories,
    previously part of the Catholic medieval Serbian Empire, by the Ottoman
    Empire several hundred years earlier, and the subsequent conversion of
    their formerly Christian population to Islam (Malcolm, 1996).

14. In research on the neurophysiological correlates of empathy, the
    psychophysiological markers as well as the neuro-images of emotions
    generated through evoking situations that had triggered fear or anger in
    the subjects are similar to the ones obtained through asking the subjects
    to recall experiences of that type they have witnessed but that happened
    to others (Preston, Bechera, Grabowski, Damasio, & Damasio, 2007).

15. To this may be added that acts of cruelty—those that produce intention-
    ally physical or emotional suffering on others, with indifference or plea-
    sure on the part of those who inflict them—have been condoned, if not
    officially endorsed, by different cultures, ours included, through wars,
    public punishment, rites of sacrifice, or entertainment, all of them ubiq-
    uitous throughout the history of humanity (Nell, 2006).

16. Newspapers report with some frequency and substantial headings
    scenarios of pedestrians passing by a seemingly homeless person lying
    on a pavement until somebody stops and tries to talk with that person,
    discovers that he is unconscious, and phones an ambulance, or the clean-
    ing personnel of an emergency room sweeping around somebody appar-
    ently sleeping in a corner of the waiting room until later that person
    slides to the floor, unconscious. Those headings and notes go on to
    lament the indifference or lack of solidarity of the many, and the exem-
    plary nature of the few, a narrative that acts as a social reminder of the
    moral imperative of minding each other.

17. Another example can be the 1938 scene that I described in my comments
    to Bigliani (Chapter Three) that has as one of its characters an uncle of
    mine in Vienna.

18. This difference is even more apparent in the Spanish language, which has
    two very distinct verbs, "ser," in reference to fixed traits ("Soy moro-
    cha"—I am a brunette) and the temporary "estar" ("Estoy cansado"—I am
    tired.), both of which conflate in translation into the English verb "to be".

19. In the field of family therapy, that distinction appears in the recommen-
    dation I heard from the Italian psychiatrist and family therapist Mara
    Selvini Palazzoli in many of her presentations to avoid using psychiatric
    labels as nouns ("He is a schizophrenic") but only as a description of
    behaviours ("He presents a schizophrenia-like behaviour") so as to

reduce immanent labels, more hopeless—both for the therapist and for the patient—and difficult to peel off. To gauge the power of labelling, see also the extraordinary 1962 experiment detailed in "Pygmalion in the classroom" (Rosenthal & Jacobson, 1992).

20. Not too long ago, it was taken for granted that those who win a war had the right to plunder, rape, and kill at will the civilian population of the newly occupied cities or regions, with impunity. Even though those practices are still enacted across many recent and present "small wars", the mere emergence of international tribunals, such as the International Criminal Court, *ad hoc* International Courts, and Truth and Reconciliation Commissions, acts as a moderator, or at least a reminder, that may reduce violation of international norms of human rights.

21. Along the lines of the red letter "A" (for Adulterous) that the noble main character was forced to display embroidered on her jacket in Nathaniel Hawthorne's moralising novel *The Scarlet Letter* (Hawthorne, 1850). In that story, as well, the protagonist endures with dignity her secret and the mark of the social affront, while the one protected by her silence tortures himself and wastes away.

22. A previous discussion of these therapeutic considerations may be found in Sluzki, 2006.

23. This latter variable—the capacity of the perpetrator to introduce disparaging remarks that propose a reversal of the responsibility for the perpetration, obfuscating the process and increasing the malignance of a violent situation—is discussed in detail in Sluzki, 1993.

24. I intentionally used the word "swallowed", which was the street word used in Argentina during the period of political repression to refer to the process of kidnapping and "disappearing" an individual.

CHAPTER FIVE

Comment III

Carlos Guillermo Bigliani

Sluzki reminds us that living in society requires the construction of an identity characterised, among other things, by a selection of behaviours that should avoid the emergence of unpleasant social emotions in the subject and in others, and should maximise instead the emergence of pleasant social emotions.

In this context (which might evoke the dynamics of pleasure-displeasure described by psychoanalysis), Carlos asks us—in an endnote—to reflect on the notion of the social construction of the "self" (Mead, 1982) and on its corollary, labelling theory. This theory deals with the impact of negative descriptive prophesies foretold by others on the construction of the subjects' identities.

It is worth remembering, at this point, that, to Aulagnier, a close follower of Freud, the path to identity is a continual process influenced by all meaningful bonds that persists throughout life. In her view, the ego is constituted by a number of identifications, which are a product of the statements made by significant others, and also of the representations offered by the gaze these others propose to the child's ego, thus consolidating his identifying construction[1] (cf. Hornstein, 2008, pp. 29–75).

According to recent views of a link-based conception of psychoanalysis (as I point out in my chapter in this book), the construction of subjectivity as a permanent process is also influenced by the imposition of the others on the subject. This version of psychoanalysis proposes the existence of multiple identities, different for every person with whom we connect.[2] This conception reinforces the possibility of thinking about conflicts in the ego as well as facilitating our work with them. Referring to conflicts in the ego, and considering the identification structure as an open system, Hornstein (2008) mentions Walt Whitman's famous lines: "Do I contradict myself? / Very well, then I contradict myself / (I am large, I contain multitudes.)".[3]

In this way, the construction of a subject through his current connections with other external subjects becomes more central. Thus, we are expanding the classic conception of the subject which a faulty comprehension of the theory freezes in a "ready made" post-Oedipal subject ruled exclusively by his relationship with his early internal objects.

The model highlighted by Carlos was always present in psychoanalysis; it is the theoretical substratum that makes it possible to think of change through treatment. Because if the subject were not capable of re-structuring through his current connections, the whole therapeutic chapter should be deleted from theory, and psychoanalysis would become exclusively a theory of being and not of changing through interaction with the present. From this angle, psychoanalysis may be considered a search for the motives opposing or hindering therapeutic change.

Carlos develops this latter dimension, the therapeutic one, applied to humiliation and shame. He proposes a creative model for a partially structured therapeutic intervention, aimed at modifying the suffering of the ego caused by these emotions. He explores the ethical, political, and religious issues entwined in these dynamics, which characterise the ties of subjects, families, and nations.

Next, I wish to add only a few comments raised by my reading of his chapter.

When dealing with the development of a shared reality and the struggle to obtain privileged positions, Sluzki points out how the battle for the role of victim has a fundamental role in interpersonal, institutional, and international narratives.

There are many clinical situations where this kind of dispute acquires specific dimensions that are worth taking into account in the process of planning therapeutic interventions as well as in open (not planned) psychoanalytic processes in which the analyst responds to the patient's free associations with a special form of listening called "floating attention". This listening is based on the clinical experience of the therapist, shaped by his own history, by the therapeutic experiences he has had as well as those performed on others, and the conclusions drawn from them and by his theoretical models. The preconscious knowledge of some configurations frequently found in his clinical work facilitates successful interventions.

We shall examine some of them.

1. In cases of symptoms of melancholy due to serious affective illnesses or bipolar disorders, we find a special kind of victimisation phenomenon: Freud (1914c) describes that a patient, supposedly the perpetrator of victimisation, accuses himself of having hurt his loved ones, but careful analysis shows an unconscious dynamic in which the patient feels he is a victim of the ill-treatment he says he has caused to others. This melancholic self-accusation, which, in his article, Freud calls melancholic self-humiliation, is a form of victimisation that is often part of a psychiatric set of symptoms, resistant to psychotherapeutic techniques and requiring urgent psychiatric intervention. The psychodynamic comprehension of the pattern does not necessarily imply that it can be modified exclusively through psychotherapy. A woman, a relative of well-known psychoanalysts, used to accuse herself of having had her husband buried in one cemetery when she should have had him buried in another. This was during a monothematic depression treated for a long time with all types of psychotherapy without success. An understanding of the unconscious dynamic of the pattern suggested it was a case of topically transformed victimisation: the patient unconsciously felt she was a victim of her husband, who should not have been with the dead but among the living, and accused him (through her self-accusation) of having deserted her. Her condition improved when a young resident doctor, unaware of her family relationship to prominent psychoanalysts, prescribed electro-convulsive therapy while the patient's therapist was on holiday.

    Far from wanting to expound on the wonders of that treatment by including this example, I intend only to recover one of the virtues of science especially advocated by Freud for psychoanalysis: to know its limits and its range of possibilities, which generally excludes depressions resistant to psychotherapy and psychopharmacological treatment.

2. In the period following an induced abortion, many couples contend for the role of privileged victim and in the hidden determinants of that dispute it is relatively frequent to find identifications with the aborted foetus in both members of the couple. This is a form of expression of unconscious dynamics where there are fantasies of filicide, which, due to the consequent guilt, after the abortion has occurred, are projected to the other member of the couple. The systematic interpretation of the fantasies may facilitate a way out of the dynamic of reciprocal victimisation, both in individual treatment and in treatment of the couple. Research shows us that it is not infrequent to find, years later, that the couple still contends for the role of victim, and this has its roots in an episode usually remote in chronological time, but present in the time of the unconscious and of the patients' symptoms.

3. Finally, another configuration would correspond to the psychopathology and treatment of subjects who have been victims of contextually generated traumatic situations, from rape to terrorism and wars, such as those described by Sluzki in his chapter.

Thus, we sketch out a wide range of situations in which the *individual*, which sometimes involves a dominant organic factor that might mainly need the help of biological psychiatry, the *interpersonal* (the case of the couple is one of many possible examples), and the *contextually traumatic* may compose a host of situations of victimisation which require different treatments. Victimisation should, then, be analysed in its complexity and it is the function of the therapist to evaluate the relative importance of those factors, highlight the dominant ones, and understand how the levels intertwine in order to guide his intervention.

Later, when Carlos deals with negative social emotions, he offers a vision not usually taken into account of the positive aspects of guilt in respect to its "social value as an incentive to corrective actions".[4] Evidently, the author does not ignore the other aspects of guilt, its oppressive, paralysing, and enslaving character. Perhaps we should remember a classic difference within psychoanalysis—in the Kleinian tradition—which makes a distinction between persecutory guilt and depressive guilt, the latter being the one with the possibility of making amends.[5] This distinction would show its twofold dimension and would set forth hypotheses about certain "corrective actions" of social value, performed by the subjects.

When he moves on to the direction of the process of change in the therapeutic context, Carlos sets forth a structure of the passage from situations of shame to emotional states involving humiliation (and vice versa). He intends to rescue the ego, which is being submitted to negative feelings and self-accusations through a change in direction. A psychoanalytical reading would redefine these labels in terms of a passage from a melancholic situation to a paranoid state, and, like all changes, it would be considered positive at first. Changes in the course of therapy, as well as spontaneous ones, allow the therapist to think there is a chance to process passages from one structure to the other, which does not mean that they will go in the correct direction, but at least they are possible. We can see the difference in the case of the woman whose condition would not change and who was treated by a resident doctor.

I have made use of this way of externalising aggressive feelings in the course of my clinical practice, specifically in treating families with relatives who were kidnapped by criminals. In general, they feel overwhelmed by guilt and shame for not having been able to look after their loved ones properly. In addition, they must face having to pay a ransom, or not paying it immediately, frequently following the negotiator's instructions. In cases like these, it is important to facilitate a change from this melancholic self-accusing position towards situations in which the group or the individual let themselves become, in their fantasy, relentless pursuers, freely expressing their wishes for revenge: "When all this is over we will put an end to the evils of these people who have humiliated us", etc.

I will now comment briefly on Carlos's techniques to promote change in the course of his therapeutic processes. In his articles on technique, Freud describes the therapeutic process using as an analogy a methodological distinction proposed by Leonardo da Vinci to distinguish orientations or categories in the fine arts. Leonardo differentiates those characterised by the methods *a levare* (as in sculpture, where parts of the material are removed to let the shape in the block of marble come into view) and *a porre* (as in painting, where the materials, for instance the colour pigments, are put on the picture).

In the first case presented by Carlos, where the subject goes from shame to humiliation, interventions seemed to be *a porre*. It is worth mentioning that, at present, analysts resort more and more frequently to variations of the classical method, offering narratives to their patients, stories destined to enrich the symbolic universe that has been impoverished in alexithymics or in children who are deeply trauma- tised due to a long hospital stay, or in the treatment of adolescents. This shows a refreshing new trend within the field of psychoanalysis.

In the second example, however, we seem to be faced with processes of the classic psychoanalytical mould: *a levare*. That is, in the course of free association produced by the patient, there are dreams. As in a classic dream of traumatic neurosis, these dreams allow us through interpretation to cause to reappear, through the marble of repetition, a piece of forgotten memory which gives rise to a new meaning that reorganises and sheds light upon the entire symptomatic life of the patient.

Through this clinical and theoretical work, Carlos recovers, enriches, and specifies Pichon Rivière's proposal for the construction of conceptual, referential, and operative schemes (a reminder of ECRO, the acronym formed from the initial letters for these words in Spanish, which included general notions about narcissism, triangular situations, resistance to change, etc.) for the feelings of humiliation and shame. According to that author, these schemes would facilitate the task of the therapist in his clinic interventions.

The presentation or explication of very abstract hypothetical con- structions such as *repetition compulsion*[6] (expressed perhaps in the "persistence" or the "systemic cohesion" Carlos refers to), or *traumatic theory*, both fuelling the clinical–therapeutic theories proposed by that author, could reinforce the essentials of this proposal (at least for the psychoanalysts' comprehension!). Maybe Carlos will not find the suggestion useful, but from the point of view of an analyst accus- tomed to what Freud called "our mythology", which is a number of meta-theories with a high degree of abstraction that would account for many terms used in the communication of clinical facts, that might round out our understanding. But I am afraid it would be trying to turn our colleague into someone more psychoanalytical than he intends to be in his chapter.

The text commented on here moves freely between understanding the symptom and interpreting the culture. The cases of the victimisation of a subject and the narratives of "belated" participants in the American Civil War, the present inhabitants of the American north and south, lead the author to the same interpretative care, whether discussing changes in their processes or their difficulty in making changes. It is important to point out the pathologic processes (denial, mania, or paranoia) involving whole nations, in which an attempt to find a way out of humiliation and shame plays a fundamental role in the commitment of whole populations to delirious, psychopathic, or paranoid leaders. We see such examples in the support the people gave to Hitler in post-Versailles Germany, the support many Argentineans granted to the dictatorial government whom they despised due to the repressive system and their "dirty war", when they decided abruptly on a senseless invasion of the Malvinas (Falklands) Islands, or the popular support received by President Bush for his invasion of Iraq after the attack on the World Trade Center (Norris, 2007).

On this topic, it is worth bearing in mind the efforts made by the Kennedy administration in order to avoid situations which would humiliate their Soviet opponents during the increasingly critical situations that led to the naval blockade in Cuba. Officials wanted to prevent subsequent escalation and the taking of revenge. Steinberg (1991) says,

> humiliation appears as a recurring theme in deterrence failures. Some of these failures have been characterized by the challenger's determination to avoid continued feelings of humiliation, i.e. Egypt's initiation of war against Israel in 1973 and Argentina's attack on the Falkland Islands in 1983. (p. 65)

This would happen regardless of the appraisal the countries may make of their own military capacity. Steinberg mentions the Yom Kippur War in 1973 and the Falklands War in 1982. There might be important similarities between these narcissistic phenomena at the international level and the narcissistic offences behind symmetrical animosities in couples.

Notes

1. It is interesting to note the similarities between this conception and the one discussed in another context (Laing, Phillipson, and Lee, 1966) in a

book that attracted both Sluzki's and my attention and launched me nearly forty years ago into the field of research in psychiatry, under his supervision. At that time, we were exploring the effects on the patients' identity of their ideas about what the staff doctors thought of them. We tried to establish correlations with what the doctors actually thought about them and, in turn, what they thought their patients thought about them as individuals. We presented the results of this research project at a professional congress quite a while ago, but, alas, they have disappeared, along with many other things, in one of our migrations.

2. "A split ego is produced on the basis of identification, a multiple ego is produced on the basis of imposition", says Berenstein as he theorises on a mechanism of subject constitution which he calls imposition. "The subject is supported by the sense of belonging inherent to the link and by the identity inherent to the ego" (2005, p. 32, translated for this edition).

3. Walt Whitman (1860) "Song of Myself", in Whitman (2008).

4. Talking with Asian colleagues, I often heard that suicide in Japan is generally the result of shameful situations in the public eye, such as a failure when trying to enter university, or the disclosure of a case of embezzlement in a bank, whereas in the West, suicide is often a sequel to guilt, regardless of whether it has been made public or not. I have no information to confirm this thesis, which might be merely the opinion of my colleagues.

Basak (2009), when he reflects on Japanese psychology, takes into account the traditional difference proposed by Morrison (1989) between shame that "generates concealment for fear of returning to the unacceptable self" and guilt which "asks for confession and forgiveness". From this perspective, he considers that in Japan "the generally expected social rule is that a woman should acquire the quality of shame, while a man must acquire the quality of guilt" (p. 275).

5. Klein, in her unique comprehension of the subjectivising process, describes two successive periods, which she identified as the paranoid–schizoid position and the depressive position, which would be fixation points for behaviours and pathologies. This perspective (Grinberg, 1964) supposes feelings of guilt in the first period, which he calls persecutory guilt: the object attacked, usually for having deprived the infant, is the same one that fed him, but in this phase he does not realise that. After the attack, the guilt urges the destruction of the object and leads to a paranoid relationship with it. In the depressive position, feelings of depressive guilt arise: the infant realises that there is a unity with the attacked object (the same one who deprived him also fed him), and this

guilt causes depressive experiences creating a reparatory activity in the infant.

6. Many authors warn us against the dangers of making these theories absolute, so that we do not fall into mechanic uses that might impoverish treatment, for example, by guiding the therapist exclusively to the reading of repetition and blinding him to what is new.

CHAPTER SIX

Comment IV

Rodolfo Moguillansky

A s Guillermo Bigliani has done, now it is my turn to elaborate on psychoanalysis and, in doing so, I will intend to provide a counterpoint to Carlos Sluzki's systemic approach. While never attempting to conceal differences, in this book we wish to build bridges between agreements and disagreements, composing a canon where all voices are clearly heard.

It is also my purpose to shed light on some "aporias" at the point where psychoanalysis and the systemic approach intersect, and also between hypotheses that seek the origin of meanings in the intrapsychic and those which find it in interaction. I use the Greek word *aporia* because various theories have caused the elaboration of some unfortunate declarations that make mutual enrichment of the models impossible. This difference generates two contradictory paradigms: psychoanalytic and systemic.

I believe that psychoanalysis cannot afford to ignore the intelligent and sharp contributions of one of the most interesting thinkers of the twentieth century, Gregory Bateson, one of the creators of systemic developments, and of some of his brilliant followers, Sluzki included. Neither do I believe that a concept that allows us to understand what is human should leave out the contributions of psychoanalysis to the "psychic reality" of each subject. This would be viewing it as a "black box" about which we know nothing.

I shall divide my comments into two parts: first, "Variations on the intrapsychic and on interaction", second, "The role of others in the narratives we build".

Variations on the intrapsychic and on interaction

Largo

As the reader will remember, after recounting the story he describes as "faintly sentimental but very moving", Sluzki suggests we discuss the emotional sequence that can be attributed to the composer–conductor at the sequence that starts with the audience's laughter. The poor man, baffled, stops conducting the orchestra and displays in sequence two very different but connected feelings:

- He glares at the audience, displaying a feeling of humiliation, where the source of the problem is external ("With your laughter you have robbed me of my finest hour!").
- He moves on to shame, where the source of the experience is internalised in a distressing self-reproach ("Swallow me, earth! I am the cause of my own failure!").

In other words, in this sequence at first the problem is externalised ("With your laughter . . .!") to pass on to shame, where the source of the experience is internalised ("Swallow me, earth . . .!").

The essence of these statements is centred on showing, very cleverly, an unstable balance between our experience of personal identity (our self), with a certain consistency of values, ethics, and behaviours, and our tendency towards social connections, attachment, and dependency on the eyes of the other.

To give conceptual depth to his line of argument, Sluzki defines "identity" as the result of what Laing, Phillipson, and Lee (1966) called "the spiral of reciprocal perspectives": my image of myself, my image of you, my image of your image of me, and so on, and he remarks then that the double process of introspection and projection constitutes our identity-in-society, in which the behaviours of the others are cause and effect of many of our conducts, in a *fusion with our significant personal social network* (the italics are mine) and even with the anonymous other when he becomes a witness to our conducts and vicissitudes or when we witness theirs—as happens with our sympathetic anguish towards the Vietnamese girl running naked along the nearly deserted road while she cries in pain and fear, her body burnt by napalm.

In his desire to show to what degree we are determined by others, he states that we want (need) to be accepted, esteemed, acknowledged for our virtues by key witnesses, as well as in many instances we want (need) to be rejected or condemned by those witnesses whose approval would ally us with those whom we disdain. This process is orientated, at a certain level, by our cognitive processes, and at another level, by a group of *social emotions*, which are signals of pleasure or of alarm that measure our behaviours, informing us of the approval (or the prediction of the approval) or the disapproval of the others (or the risk of it), using as an indicator the contrast between how we wish to be seen and how the public eye sees us.

The causal line described by Sluzki in his vignette continues in a second act, that is, the public display of shame, an emotion usually expressed in private, or concealed, dramatically increases the possibility that the audience might empathise with the conductor (it makes him "human"), which generates the growing discomfort—the feeling of guilt—as a result of the audience's previous behaviour. In the third act, the noble attitude of the conductor acts as a catalytic agent: the audience, which so far did not know what to do in their uneasiness, identifies with him. He displays reparatory behaviour, which then becomes a collective action and helps to put an end to the collective feeling of guilt.

After the introduction, Sluzki comments, "The complex task of living in society requires us to be permeable to the opinions and expectations of the other members of the collective of which we are a part. (Reciprocally, we assume that they will be sensitive to our own opinions and expectations.)" He also tells us that this capacity allows us to plan, assess, and perfect our social actions through our perception and our assumption of the impact we generate on others. In general, we adapt our relationship to the surrounding social world and minimise the risk of unbalance.

I can only agree with the emphasis on the role played by the setting in establishing our way of thinking and acting, but at this point, and to continue with my comment, I must make a method-ological digression to introduce some nuances in the basic agreement.

Adagio

This second movement in my variations, with the slow quality of the adagio, is devoted to a theoretical–methodological digression, includ-ing some comments that I am sure are shared by Sluzki.

The framework

Every approach defines a framework with a certain kind of landscape, and prescribes a particular look or way of listening as well as a way to operate in it. Thus, in all disciplines, the framework defines a border that delimits space and time, which contains what we see and, at the same time, suggests what has been left outside it. The look and the mode of listening delimited by each approach within its particu-lar framework only draw a possible map of the landscape explored; they do not encompass the whole territory.[1]

There is no such thing as total knowledge

With each approach we do not build a "map" that contains, as Borges' The Aleph[2], the total sum of all knowledge and all views. Conse-quently, I suggest that every theory that assumes it is possible to include all angles, which endeavours to be a general psychology able to explain simultaneously all determinations of the human world, is sure to fall into reductionism sooner or later.

What is the span of the framework proposed by psychoanalysis?

The proposals of psychoanalysis, from my perspective, do not span all human life. They only deal with the way in which we are determined by "the unconscious", and they only open a "window" to listen to those determinations.[3]

One of the merits of that window is that it questions the illusion towards which the human gaze is inertly directed. The human gaze is allergic to enduring opacities, discontinuities, or nonsense, and to creating a field for tolerating them and thinking about them: this implies the possibility of bearing the abandonment of *illusion* in an all-embracing gaze (Moguillansky, 2003, 2004; Steiner, 1974).

On occasion, psychoanalysis ignores the fact that the listening it allows refers only to the map it encompasses with its methods, and unwisely turns its findings into ontological truths,[4] truths that endeavour to refer to all that is human.

The look of psychoanalysis and the systemic look:
the intrapsychic and the interactional

In this respect, Guillermo Bigliani says in his chapter that as a reaction to the hyper-valuation of the intrapsychic (*put forward by psychoanalysis*), in the early 1950s, a pragmatic and creative conception arose which emphasised the analysis of interactions and systems of which the subjects were a part, as being the main determinants of psychopathology, putting aside intrapsychic determinants. The latter were part of a black box whose mechanism was not unknown to most of the authors, but they decided not to include it in their theorisations.

We do not see what we do not see

What do we see? Do we see that which we do not see? This is not a minor problem for any reflection on this issue. Von Foerster, in "Vision, language and knowledge: the double blind" (2002), reminds us that in monocular vision there is a blind spot corresponding to what should be seen by the receptors supposedly placed in the eye. Foerster says that not only do we not see, but that we also do not know that we do not see. He calls this a second-order dysfunction. Von Foerster suggests that the different levels of language allow us to accede to different visions of the world, or, more emphatically, they allow us to accede to different worlds.

Andante

After this disquisition, I shall continue with my comment on Chapter Four.

At the end of his story about the composer, Sluzki recounts that the audience goes from exchanging humorous comments to awkward whispering, which turns into absolute silence when they notice the regular, highly respected conductor in the proscenium. Standing up, he takes off his tailcoat, and, in his shirt sleeves, waistcoat, and braces, addresses the composer, who is still sitting on the platform crying, and asks him loudly and respectfully, "Please, maestro, continue!" In answer to this, the men in the audience take off their jackets while they all applaud. The applause of the public and the orchestra brings him out of his misery. He looks around; he sees the conductor, the orchestra, and the audience, who are applauding in their shirtsleeves. He pulls himself together, stands up, and, baton in hand, starts conducting the orchestra again in his successful debut.

We may agree that this happy ending entails the possibility that the composer can listen to the conductor's *"Please maestro, continue!"* and understand it as an empathic gesture of encouragement.

It might not have been the case, in spite of the regular conductor's kind tone.

- This external source, this "kind tone", might have been felt by the composer as a repetition of his childhood experiences with a father who scorned him when he had to face difficulties. So, he would have conferred the attributes of his scornful father on the conductor (Freud, 1909b). In this case, "the corrective emotional experience" made possible by the conductor's words would not have had the desired effect.[5]
- He might—from his childhood rivalry with his father, for whom, in the Oedipal drama, he felt hate and whose vengeful retaliation he feared—not consider "the regular conductor" good (Freud, 1909b) but look upon his attitude as an aggressive and scornful act, following Klein's logic (1946) regarding the paranoid reaction, making it impossible for him to acknowledge the kindness of the conductor, which forces him to assume his previous hatred.
- He might, if he thought in terms of an epistemology tinged with *misconceptions*, consider the kind gesture of the conductor as trying to show his superiority (Money-Kyrle, 1961).[6]

I could go on and on with versions in which the production of sense has its origins in psychic reality.

To my mind, Sluzki offers such versions when he examines the role of others in the generation of what he calls negative emotions, and so considers that *personal variants such as anxiety levels in a basic state (or, a personal tendency to feel calm or anxious before new situations, which is the same thing) have interpersonal effects: anxious people generate anxiety, which increases the possibility of misunderstandings and arguments. Besides, they are not able to distinguish between trustworthy persons and those who are not to be trusted, which in turn increases the probability of their ending up as victims in the social exchange. Something similar may be said about other personal variables, such as impulsiveness: the probability of becoming a perpetrator increases in this case.*

I have the impression that in these descriptions, Sluzki places the origin of the sequence in that which psychoanalysts call psychic reality. He even points out that when shame acquires a dominant position in the subject's vision of the world, his self-esteem is impaired as his ability as an actor diminishes. His voice does as well, for he has become a puppet of social rules. Psychic reality, in my opinion, acquires an important role in his approach when he explores the anticipatory emotion of shame. In his description, he says it constitutes a key guide to sociality and also to morality, "a gyroscope that signals possible transgressions—both past, as a learning experience, and future, as an alarm signal—and, therefore, acts as a prelude, if not as a key component, of what we call conscience".

This is reinforced when he refers to "externalisation" and "internalisation", in which personal styles depend on psychical defence mechanisms as described by Freud, or more substantially by Klein, as well as the prevalence of "disruptive, aggressive, destructive, and, broadly speaking, antisocial behaviours, or the prevalence of "anxious and depressive behaviours". These considerations lead him to say that "purity", granted by interactions of the role of victim and perpetrator, varies according to the circumstances.

It is in the explanation of personal variables that my opinion differs most from his. He says that these are the outcome of elementary situations that threaten the stability of a relationship, or they are neurobiological variables in perpetrators and victims. While I will not deny the value of the elementary situations that threaten the stability of a relationship or that of the neurobiological variables, I would place the emphasis on the relationship between a subject and his own system of ideals.

With regard to the subject, there are vast differences from individual to individual regarding the tendencies of anticipation or involving oneself in situations that might generate reactions of shame or humiliation. So, one situation can trigger one or the other emotion in different subjects given the same circumstances, on the assumption of a combination of traumatic experiences and predispositions (vulnerabilities, idiosyncrasies with a genetic origin). This is the so-called stress–diathesis hypothesis that attempts to explain why the same circumstances generate such diverse emotions in different people. Many authors have demonstrated the importance of genetic components in relevant dimensions of our disposition (Buss & Plomin, 1984; Goldsmith, 2003; Plomin & Caspi, 1998). Different family traits appear associated in children in whom there is a predominant social experience of shame (i.e., an internalisation of negativity) or of humiliation (i.e., an externalisation of negativity): families with rigid or chaotic ways of functioning, characterised by global attributions, affective distance, humiliation as a way of disapproval, the use of "love" as reward/punishment. And there is a great deal of research to assert that these traits persist from childhood to adulthood (Caspi, Elder, & Bem, 1987, 1988; Dennissen, Asendorpf, & van Aken, 2008). Summing up, diversified by genetic proclivities and varied life experiences, we carry with us a set of internalised "witnesses" who make an essential contribution to what we vaguely call moral conscience, an "internalised cacophony": our parents, our relatives, our teachers, our confessors, leaders who pass judgement on our actions with comments and advice that is sometimes kind and gentle, sometimes lenient and forbearing, sometimes strict or even sadistic and degrading, echoing external voices in agreement with everyday or exceptional experiences.

Allegro

It can also be said that psychoanalysis itself has considered that we are not determined solely by our internal world; our environment also institutes us. Laing and Esterson (1967) related research on families who had at least one "schizophrenic" member, showing that the clinically symptomatic behaviour of schizophrenia was a dramatic adaptation to family conditions. The same can be said of Wynne, Ryckoff, Day, and Hirsch in their text, "Pseudo-mutuality in the family relations of schizophrenics" (1958), where they asserted that "in pseudo-mutuality the emotional participation tends more to maintain the sense of fulfilment of reciprocal expectations than to actually perceive the changing expectations". Pseudo-mutuality implied a typical dilemma: divergence was perceived in these families as a disruption of the relationship, so it had to be avoided. But if it was avoided it could not grow, and a peculiar variety of shared family mechanisms were developed, by means of which the acknowledgement of deviations regarding role structure was avoided, or they were reinterpreted in a delirious way.

These shared mechanisms work at a primitive level, preventing the articulation and selection of any meaning which would allow the individual member to differentiate his personal identity, within or without the family role structure, so that the incipient perceptions and communications that might lead to an articulation of expectations, interests, or diverging individualities were cancelled, shaded, or distorted.

In "The interfamilial environment of the schizophrenic patient: the transmission of irrationality" (Lidz, Cornelison, Fleck, & Terry, 1957), Lidz and his team state that

the boundaries of the environment set by the parents, and their perception of facts destined to meet their needs, bring about a strained family atmosphere to which children must adapt themselves to meet the dominant need, or else feel rejected.

Because of this "irrationality", facts are constantly altered to adapt to emotionally determined needs. The world the child should come to perceive or feel is denied to him and the acceptance of mutually contradictory experiences requires paralogic thinking; the environment, according to this perspective, trains the child in irrationality.

Since the 1960s, psychoanalysis has paid considerable attention to the role of interaction between individuals and their relationship with others and with the social imaginary. The CEFRAP (Centre for French Studies in Training and Active Research on the dynamic psychology of personality and human groups) was created in Paris for this reason, under the leadership of Didier Anzieu. Also, in those years, Pontalis (1963) gave theoretical support to the new practices when he published his emblematic work "Le petit groupe comme objet" (The small group as object).

Kaës (1976) continued and elaborated on the work begun by Pontalis (1963) and Anzieu and Martin (1965), the first authors in France to wonder whether the group is or is not an object of psychoanalysis. Later contributions provided better tools for this expansion of the solipsistic horizon originally proposed by psychoanalysis.

Aulagnier's conception of the "narcissistic contract" (1975), based on Castoriadis's concept of the instituting role of the "Social imaginary" (Castoriadis, 1975), described the operation by means of which each person is subjected to the prevailing values in a given culture.

Kaës (1993), in turn, acknowledges the relationship between the individual and his environment, stating that the group holds the individual through a matrix of roles, caring, recognitions, fulfilments, means of protection and of attack, and clear boundaries, hierarchies, representations, and prohibitions.

Presto: "Neither too much nor too little"

I do not intend to question the importance of the milieu to us and our impact on it. What I am doing is playing down the role of that reciprocal influence when we try to understand the sources of shame and humiliation. I assume that Sluzki shares my point of view about clarifying the determination of reciprocal perspective spirals.

However, I do not share Lacan's proposition when he affirms "Il n'y a pas de rapport sexuel".[7] This may be understood as "there are sexual relations, but there is no sexual proportion", or, in other words, there is no proportion between one's action and the other's, which extends to refer to the lack of proportion between one's behaviour and the other's feeling and response.

I would also add that what we are is not simply the answer to the environment's attitude towards us. From my perspective, I would suggest it is necessary to clarify how we are influenced according to the "spiral of reciprocal perspectives" proposed by Laing, Phillipson, and Lee (1966): it does not do to consider the intrapsychic a black box or to cast aside the determinant role of the spiral of reciprocal perspectives.

I shall now return to the framework issue. Each framework, together with the theory it implies, allows us to listen, see, and give priority to certain determinations at the expense of others. We must also pay attention to see that which the framework excludes (von Foerster, 2002).

When psychoanalysis does not take into account that self-preservation is being set aside because of the framework, it is creating a blind spot where the role of reciprocal spirals is not seen. Likewise, if we only pay attention to the reciprocal spirals, we run the risk of missing the determinations provided by the subjectivity of each individual.

The role of others in the narratives we build

In this second part, I shall not divide my contribution into "movements"; instead I shall introduce comments to establish correspondences and dissonances to provide a counterpoint in this exciting dialogue with Sluzki.

In his chapter, Carlos discusses the role of the others in the creation or generation of shameful or humiliating situations. Throughout the text this question arises: who are the actors on the stage in the situations that generate experiences of shame and humiliation? In order to explore the issue in the narratives we build, he clearly defines "victims", "witnesses", and "perpetrators".

I think Sluzki would agree that the narratives we build actually create the world in which we live, that the human world is a human construction, that language does not represent the world; in this sense language has a formative aspect: when we say something we are not merely giving a name to something, we are calling it into being. Gadamer (1975) affirms that we are immersed in language, there is nothing outside it, or, if there is, we cannot possibly grasp it. This reference to language is similar to that of Wittgenstein (1922). According to Wittgenstein, language builds different possible worlds.

Sluzki emphasises, with great clinical richness, that those who define themselves as victims and those who define themselves as perpetrators build different narratives. So, this is important information when we plan any therapeutic activity. He believes therapeutic work habitually focuses on the reorganisation of events and the negative emotions that weigh them down, with the intention of reducing the polarity of discrepancies, redistributing responsibilities, and somehow increasing the possibility of reparation and/or significance.

He states it is essential to study negative emotions, particularly shame and humiliation. The semiology he proposes of these "negative" emotions is very interesting.

- They are generally avoided.
- If perceived, they are usually neutralised.
- They are unpleasant or uncomfortable, and as they generate "negative feedback", they trigger behaviours intended to reduce or correct the deviation.
- They are self-referential, although they require the presence of at least one person, real or virtual, who points out a difference between how we wish to be perceived and judged and how (we believe) we are perceived and judged. If we consider the abasement of the image the others might have of us, our self-esteem might be diminished.

In this rich semiology, Sluzki tells us about the subjective side, how each person deals with these negative emotions: (a) they are generally avoided (psychoanalysts would say "repressed"); (b) they are usually neutralised (psychoanalysts believe that in the attempt we develop inhibitions); (c) they are perceived as unpleasant. This unpleasantness would be considered by a psychoanalyst to be a non-agreement of the ego with its own internal system of ideals; (d) they are self-referential.

With regard to self-reference, Aulagnier (1975) has stated that primary functioning,[8] which invades the secondary logic with which the ego intends to operate, occurs according to the premise that everything that happens to us is conceived by us as the effect of the "omnipresent wish of the other". This way of thinking about that which hurts us has the Pyrrhic advantage of making us believe that everything that happens in the world which does not suit us is destined for us, and is habitual when dealing with negative emotions. Even though it "diminishes our self-esteem", it is difficult to think of a world that in general is not "doing things to us", and this hurts us worse than supposing there is a black hand lurking about and doing us harm.

Among the negative social emotions, Carlos marks out: (a) a social discomfort or embarrassment, a sort of "minor shame" and (b) two aversive social emotions which are very intense, shame and humiliation, which share the feeling of being exposed and undervalued or disgraced in public due to something we have done or have failed to do.

Then he shows the difference between: (a) the shame that appears when there is an *agreement* between the view of the public eye and the private eye, that is, there is a loss of social value in which the image the other has of us (at least what we perceive about the image the other has of us) agrees with our own assessment of our behaviour or situation; and (b) humiliation, in which, unlike the other case, the negative image of us which we attribute to the others and/or the behaviour of the others reveals that it *does not agree* with our image of the situation or action being judged. As a result, we feel accused or unfairly treated. The difference between (a) and (b) is not always clear, as shown by ambiguous words such as ignominy or dishonour.

I agree with Sluzki in his description, and I would include the role of agreement or non-agreement in our own system of ideals. In my essay, I stress the fact that in shame, the integrity of the ego is preserved, whereas in humiliation it is shattered. Sluzki asserts that shame, together with its opposite, pride, form one of the emotional bases of interpersonal relationships. Shame traps the individual in a future of failure, worthlessness, and self-rejection that tends to be felt as irreversible the moment it happens. The individual justifies the critical perception and the rejection on the part of others. The self is perceived by the subject as inferior, faulty, with no possibility of reform.

The chronic experience of shame stimulates vicious circles: (a) shame abuse (increased by loneliness, inability to defend oneself, self-contempt, or fear) and (b) shame failure (since shame reduces the efficiency of future actions, which operate as "well-learnt discouragement"). The anticipation of this possibility sustains the essence of the social function of this emotion, associated with the fear of social isolation.

I must say I find the description of the different alternatives to the subjective experience very accurate in the case of "abuse" as well as in that of "failure" and how they condition possible future benevolent interactions because, from his self, the subject will receive them with "hopelessness" or will tend to avoid them due to the retraction (inhibition) he might feel in the face of his fear of social isolation.

Sluzki defines humiliation as an emotion linked to seeing oneself or feeling that one is treated in an unfairly negative way, or even anticipating this possibility. This is associated with an experience of an attack on dignity, pride, or power, and triggers acts or fantasies of retribution or revenge.

Sluzki states that shame and humiliation—or a prediction of them—work as a rudder that guides our insertion in the social world: (a) keeping us informed as to how our behaviour is perceived by others; (b) how consonant or dissonant we sound with regard to the standards of our acquaintances, our social circumstances, and our surrounding cultural milieu; (c) to what extent our expectations and self-image agree with the signals received from our social world in that respect.

In addition, our perception is strongly influenced by our own attitude. Sluzki also considers this personal attitude when he points out that interaction is limited by personal variants such as anxiety levels in a basic state (or, which is the same thing, the personal proclivity to feel calm or anxious in regard to new situations) that have interpersonal effects in and of themselves, or the prevalence of "disruptive, aggressive, destructive, and, broadly speaking, antisocial behaviours" or the prevalence of inhibited, insecure, anxious, and depressive conducts. He implies that the more concordant the relationship between our own expectations and the signals of the social world, personal ethical norms, and the circumstantial priorities of the social context, the more those social emotions will be perceived as useful indicators for flexibility in our behaviour.

He also asserts that if they acquire dominance as universes independent of the context: (a) we become their terrified servants, oppressed by an endless number of immobilising rules that invade our self; (b) our self-evaluation and that of our context are clouded and we generate high levels of suffering, both in ourselves and in our surroundings.

I wish to comment that I am particularly interested in this issue regarding the subtle boundary between "harmony" with the values that surround us and the risk of becoming "terrified servants, oppressed by an endless number of immobilising rules that invade our self". In fact, I have devoted special attention to this point (Moguillansky, 2003, 2004; Moguillansky & Szpilka, 2009).

In several texts I have discussed the fact that in order to belong to the human community we need to be instructed by culture. In order to continue being a part of it, we need to share the same language and similar fundamental principles, but we are alienated when there is an agreement between the instructing and the instructed. The difference between what the milieu instructs and the resulting instruction makes total harmony impossible. In order not to feel alienated, in order to be free, as Sartre said (1960), we must face up to a lack of harmony with the prevailing values.

Sluzki's excellent chapter is at its best when he wonders: who are the actors who stage situations that generate experiences of shame and humiliation?

As he describes each one of the characters, he informs us, in addition to the many factors in the context that affect the kind of social emotion triggered as well as the quality and intensity of the experience, about: (a) the friendly witness. This is the one who removes our awkwardness and offers us an externalising way out, proposing that we are not to blame, that the event has occurred because of X, thus diminishing the intensity of the social emotion which comes together with the experience; (b) the hostile witness. He, on the other hand, is insensitive to our potential physical pain or to our self-esteem, and even finds them ludicrous, or, even worse, he defines the event as awkward and unbalanced. Sluzki says that the hostile witness usually drives us to react with confrontation, trying to adjust the balance, or we are left brooding over a fantasy of revenge. Hostile witnesses intensify the probability and the amount of the humiliating experience. He adds that in that context perhaps humiliation is tinged with a touch of shame if we do not dare to confront the witness who has turned our mishap into an affront; (c) the indifferent witness. He is the one who behaves as if our misfortune were not his business at all. This kind of social indifference, relatively infrequent and socially improper, may, if we tend to feel shame, drive us to be grateful that the witness acted as if he had not noticed anything, while, if we usually feel humiliated, we might define him as a hostile actor, fit to be questioned. Sluzki concludes that the "neutral witness" does not exist in practice except in cases of mediation (even though, in hostile confrontations, each party presents a version of reality and the witness is asked to be on the side of one or the other).

After these descriptions, Sluzki plays down the determining role of the witness when he tells us that if we are the kind of people who are easily ashamed—perhaps considered shy or insecure—we will certainly feel ashamed even if the witness is too kind. Whereas if we are inclined to externalise our blunders, regardless of the nature of the witness and the sort of event (we may have been diagnosed as sociopaths, or at least aggressive), then we might feel humiliated, and no Good Samaritan witness will be able to change that. In the process of building on his theme, the author discusses some scenes where the witness adds offence when he allies himself with the perpetrator and thus justifies his acts.[9] The hostile witness is then a co-perpetrator, increasing the intensity of the negative experience, while the friendly witness moderates it.

Epilogue

I would like to close my comments by repeating that it was a privilege to be able to engage in a dialogue with Carlos Sluzki at the meeting in São Paulo and in the writing of this book.

Notes

1. Bateson (1972), following Korzybski, called our attention to the relationship map territory.
2. Borges (1960) tells in his story that he saw the *Aleph* at the bottom of a dilapidated staircase in a dark cellar on Garay Street in Buenos Aires. The *Aleph* was a small iridescent sphere two centimetres in diameter, and the light it radiated was such that he first thought it was some rotating object. But it was not; it was motionless. Borges' *Aleph* was a site where we could see all places in the world unmistakably, from every angle, and in all its possible representations.
3. Laplanche states this issue in similar terms in the seminars about "The Cask" (Laplanche, 1987). He covers the seminars of 1979–1981 and 1983–1984 when he says that psychoanalysis is not a general psychology to be suspended or left aside. Psychoanalysis deals with that which is "caused by desire, by the unconscious", and it has the tools to deal with it.
4. I agree with Bertrand Russell (1914) (cf. Ferrater Mora, 1979, par. "Construction") on this issue, when he states that theories are, or should be, only "symbolically built fictions". Russell's maxim is "whenever possible, inferred entities should be replaced by constructions". Russell believed that when entities are inferred there is a tendency to populate the world ontologically.
5. The idea presented by Sluzki is similar to that of Alexander and French (1946) when they say that when the patient is exposed, under favourable circumstances, to an emotional situation which formerly he was not able to manage, the therapist temporarily assumes a particular role that helps to generate the experience and facilitate the confrontation with reality.

6. A notion created by Money-Kyrle to describe the erroneous conception of the infant by virtue of envy. Money-Kyrle says that because of envy, the child might believe that the breast feeds him to show its superiority and this misconception might influence his future vision of the world.

7. At the beginning of the Encore seminar, Lacan (1972) illustrates the topology of phallic enjoyment by means of the paradox of Achilles and the tortoise proposed by Zeno. Powerful Achilles allows the tortoise a few metres' head start and then he races after it. When he has covered the same distance as the head start, the tortoise will have gained a new head start that is certainly small, but it will not be in the same place, and the reasoning continues *ad infinitum*. So, Achilles will never overtake the tortoise. With this paradox, Lacan gives a metaphor of sexual relations (rapport). Here, the term "relation (rapport)" is used as in mathematics, a ratio, a proportion between two members.

    At every stage, the tortoise maintains its head start, related, in a way, to Achilles' race. There is no relation (rapport) because their meeting point is a limit that cannot be reached through a finite sum of proportions.

8. The primary process is the one corresponding to the way our unconscious thoughts function.

9. I discuss the experience—related to Felice, Pirandello's character—in my text in this book.

CHAPTER SEVEN

Shame, humiliation, and the hero

Rodolfo Moguillansky

> What was missing for Utopia to vanquish reality? What defeated Utopia? Why, with the pedantic superiority of converts, do many of those who were on our side, betray Utopia? Am I writing of causes or of effects? Am I writing of effects and not describing causes? Am I writing of causes and not describing effects? I am writing about the history of a lack, not about the lack of history.
>
> (Rivera, 1993, p. 57)

> The truth, so simple and yet so terrifying, is that people who in normal conditions might have perhaps dreamed of crimes but never have fostered the intention of committing them, adopted in conditions of complete tolerance of law and society an outrageously criminal behaviour.
>
> (Arendt, 1951, p. 181)

Introduction

Shame and humiliation are human emotions that play an important role in the relationship a subject has with himself as well as with others. They play a role in the adjustment each one of us makes to his self-esteem and to the assessments we feel we receive from the human community we are part of and with which we interact.

These emotions have been assessed and conceptualised in different disciplines. In this book, we intend to discuss convergences and divergences as viewed from the paradigm of psychoanalysis and using the systemic approach.

In order to develop my point of view, from a psychoanalytical perspective on humiliation and shame, I must establish that human subjectivity is a product of culture. More specifically, I must say that human subjectivity appears and is instituted at the crossroad provided by the family, who enunciates the foundations of culture, and an *infans* who, to become human, must receive those impositions and then accept them as his own. From that crossroad appears what we feel as "This is me".

The representation of our "self", that which we feel as our ego, evolves in a "new psychic act" in the shape of a self-sufficient entity (Freud, 1915c), an ego that "believes" it has everything and supposes there is nothing alien to itself.

What a psychoanalyst considers to be the "ego" is not a minor problem.

Freud (1914c) proposes that the representation of the self, which constitutes the ego, is acquired after our biological birth.

I must make it clear that I do not delimit the notions of "ego" and "self". In the notion of ego, I include both the adaptative functions (as proposed by ego psychology) and the representation of one's self, which, due to its inevitably pompous nature, forces us to ignore our errors and inadequacies (as proposed by Lacan). I maintain this duplicity, as Freud (1923b) does, because it constitutes the ego and our self, thus allowing us to explain and uphold our psychopathologic considerations.

Freud says that this initial shape of the feeling of the self, an ego, which believes it owns everything, is not feasible and is forced to change. He proposes that to be feasible, the ego must grow apart from the supposition that leads it to feel complete and self-sufficient. This conception of completion and self-sufficiency that the ego should leave behind to conceive a world alien to it with which it will have to relate will give rise to the *ideal ego*, the paradigm of the sufficiency it mythically believed it had.

In more colloquial terms, we could say that the ego at first "believed" it was "all" but then this belief could not be upheld and the *ideal ego* was constituted.

A posteriori, the ego will be ruled by the *ideal of the ego*, the site of norms and ethical and aesthetical aims that it will face.

This "ego", born and created in the process of humanisation, which has the original sin of self-sufficiency, will have to struggle with a reference system, with a set of values, in the presence of which it will feel inadequate. Freud (1914c) has proposed that the representation of the self, which constitutes the ego, is acquired after our biological birth.

The ego, then, suffers from a tortured longing for the loss of what it believed it was, which became ideal (the *ideal ego*), and it also suffers because it is not able to obey all the norms proposed by the *ego ideal*.

To accord its true importance to this proposition, it is necessary to remember that from Freud (1914c) onwards, psychoanalysis has provided all too many proofs that the human ego wishes to conceive itself as omniscient, omnipotent, and self-sufficient, and it suffers when these aims are not achieved.

Psychoanalysis distinguishes two different patterns of psychical functioning that co-exist and operate simultaneously.

- One ruled by the pleasure principle, which can be colloquially described as a hedonistic principle serving to fulfil wishes. This unconscious longing for the fulfilment of wishes usually comes into conflict with the ego, posing a dilemma: on the one hand, it tries to deal with them, on the other, it does not want to be an actor in them. The ego runs the risk of being the actor in something improper. The solutions to the compromise of the ego, by means of repression, produce the so-called formations of the unconscious: symptoms, dreams, transferences, and the psychopathology of everyday life.
- One that is beyond what is ruled by the pleasure principle, emerging at events that, due to their excessive nature, cannot be processed by the psychic apparatus, particularly by the ego within the system of the pleasure principle.

What is ruled by the logic that is beyond the pleasure principle is not meant for wish fulfilment. It gives rise to reactions of the mind that are caused by the element of surprise, by uneasiness, the danger that makes the ego feel the risk of dissolution and of losing its notion of itself.

The effects from that which is processed from within the pleasure principle and from that which is processed by the system beyond the pleasure principle are different.

Items that originate in the pleasure principle give rise to neurotic symptoms and what is processed with the logic that is beyond the pleasure principle causes narcissistic injuries to the ego.

I consider shame a painful feeling, caused by the emergence of an unwanted feeling of the ego, and it can be processed within the system of the pleasure principle.

Humiliation, instead, brings about "excessive pain", which affects the ego in its essence, leading it to function in the system that is beyond the pleasure principle.

I assert that in humiliation, the ontological status of the ego is at stake.

I will elaborate on this later, when I write about the judgement of attribution and the judgement of existence. The former signals what is "negative" for the ego within the system of the pleasure principle; the latter gives signals that hasten the appearance of that which is beyond the pleasure principle.

Once this conceptual platform is established, I shall enlarge on the discussion of one of the difficult problems of the ego, that which the ego feels or experiences as shame, and I shall also show that when this failure of the ego becomes traumatic (what psychoanalysis calls narcissistic injury), it is experienced as humiliation.

In this text, I consider the ego the locus where shame and humiliation are experienced. Therefore, I will devote a good portion of my writing to what happens to the ego in the presence of these emotions.

In my considerations on humiliation, I shall give special attention to the ego's plunging into "heroic identification" as a way to "resolve" the narcissistic injury caused by humiliation and then I shall explore other, "less heroic", ways of resolution. I shall also offer some ideas about the role of shame as one of the organisers of human behaviour in society. Finally, I shall give two examples that take different paths in the elaboration of these painful feelings.

Human subjectivity, the feeling of the self, a product of culture

Human subjectivity, a product of the crossroad where the infans *and the enunciations of the foundations imposed by culture meet*

I proposed in the introduction that the feelings we experience about our self, what psychoanalysts call the ego, originate at the crossroad produced in the meeting of the *infans* and the enunciations imposed by culture through the family.

Even though at birth we have instinctive reactions to alarm, such as the Moro reflex, humans, in the inevitable process of acculturation imposed upon us, suffer from an instinctive uprooting, so that the feelings we experience are not instinctive, pre-determined, pre-experienced reactions (as is usually considered the case for other species), with the possible exception of the reaction to pain.

The Moro reflex (also known as the startle reflex) is an automatic reaction observed in its complete form in newborns (after the thirty-fourth week of gestation), and in incomplete form in premature birth (after the twenty-eighth week of gestation). It is a response to unexpected loud noise or when the infant feels it is falling on its back.

The image of one's self is predetermined by bonds before birth

The image of one's self is predetermined by bonds that predate a person's birth; it begins to exist in the minds of the future parents. The identifications that help to constitute him find their substance in that which the parents imagined about him. (This has been affirmed by many authors, such as Aulagnier, 1975, 1984; Enríquez, 1996; Faimberg, 1988; Kaës, Faimberg, Enriquez, & Baranes, 1993; Nachin, 1995).

The subject begins to exist as an individual before he is born, in his parents' imagination, which in its turn is predetermined, of course, by culture. Once he is born, the individual is subjected to culture for his humanisation and the family plays a central role in this process. The social environment marks the relationship the parents have with the child.

Again, the social discourse projects on the *infans* the same anticipation as that which characterises the parental discourse. Long before the new subject is born, the social group anticipates the place he is supposed to have, in the hope that he will then transmit the cultural model. Thus, not only the parents but the whole of society will predetermine the locus where the newborn will be organised in interaction with his parents and with his own constitutional disposition.

The subject, in turn, will seek and find in the cultural discourse the references that will allow him to project into the future, so that the distance from his initial support, his parents, will not result in the loss of all identifying supports (Aulagnier, 1975).

In this process, a very important role is played by the extension of the social network beyond the parents and even the family, as the young child socialises with others: for example, at nursery school.

The human subject, subjected to cultural heritage, torn between the need to be an end in itself and a link in a chain

Freud (1914c) taught us that every subject is torn between the need to be an end or a link in a chain to which he is joined without having been asked. The child is marked by a struggle between organising his own identity and the duty to fulfil the unattained wishes of his parents.

Every individual is pre-determined by more than the family and social bonds existing around the time of his birth. Every individual receives a treasure trove of meanings, of knowledge, of abilities that mankind has collected, sometimes anonymously and sometimes with a name, which he uses. In that sense, we are not only heirs to the family that precedes us as well as to remote ancestors who jointly take part in the shaping of our subjectivity; we inherit multiple and diverse traditions; we are heirs to a continuum of wishes, ideals, and meanings shared by generations. This heritage passes on to us options that determine the way our individuality is constituted within the family web that precedes us and, in turn, anticipates what will happen to us. This heritage is organised into identifications.

Although obvious, it is important to point out that we can become human only if we acquire identifications that make us human. We build the identifications with the heritage received in the humanising relationship with other humans; when culture establishes us as subjects according to the rules of kinship, it creates identifications that will allow us to become human subjects. It is life together with another human being that constitutes the singularity of a subject. Every Robinson Crusoe needs his Friday in order to become human.

We relate based on them and we seek to find them in our relationship with others. Not only are we the result of identifications, but we also acquire the conflicts posed by them.

Every individual will have to process the raft of identifications that he has received, to remodel them, and from that foundation he will be able to shape his own identity, as well as anything else he may devise.

Access to the human order is linked to our participation in a reference system

As humans we are built by the cultural enunciations transmitted by our family. Therefore, we acquire references with which we will move about, notions of generation gaps, roles of father, mother, son/daughter, and rules, which prescribe and proscribe our relationship with them. In this way is the human world organised and its central organising rule is the "incest taboo". Culture institutes our way of feeling and thinking within the parameters established by kinship, it includes us in a "contract", a "narcissistic contract" (Aulagnier, 1975) to which we must adhere in order to be part of the human world.

These requirements, by establishing our way of feeling and thinking within the web created by kinship, demand that we renounce certain things instinctively (psychoanalysts would say these are repressions), which leads to the emergence of desires and feelings determined and delimited by that repression. On the one hand, repression introduces an unconscious order and, on the other, to compensate, it establishes a system of ideals which human longing wants to reach.

The ego and the ideal

From the ego we can speak, think symbolically, and acquire an image of ourselves, which allows us to feel "this is me".

The human ego is characterised by a structure made up of the enunciations it inspired and which result in identifications as well as in remodelling that the ego itself produces from them. The ego must make these identifications its own and, in order to do that, it must adopt Goethe's words (1828–1829): "if you want to inherit your parents' legacy, go and win it".

It is the ego's task to build knowledge, to generate enunciations that make its surroundings intelligible, such as the world and the relationship it has with the world.

In this perspective, reality is a set of definitions, of enunciations built by the ego and consistent in turn with the cultural discourse that has instituted the ego.

In order to create an image of reality of the world, a representation of the world, the ego transforms everything that exists into a representation consistent with its own structure. For the ego, knowing the world means being able to represent it intelligibly and to insert it within a relational scheme, which agrees with its real self. In order to be able to represent the elements it processes, the ego imposes on them the same enunciations that have constituted it. Hence, the representation of the world is a creation of the ego; it represents the relationship imposed by the ego on the elements occupying that space.

The knowledge of the ego is also knowledge of the image of its own self, of the love for its own self. In the loving relationship of the ego with itself, a major role is played by the ideal.

With regard to the ideal, psychoanalysis distinguishes:

- the *ideal ego*, the site of all perfections. The *ideal ego* appears in the child when his parents declare him an object of perfection. This idealisation takes form in the phrase "His Majesty, the baby";
- the *ideal of the ego*, as a normative reference. It becomes a reference in so far as it is the site of the social ideals that the ego must attain to receive the love of the other, also an ideal.

Both are products of the relationship with others, and beginning with others, they are internalised by each subject. In its relationship with the two forms of ideals, the ego is forever subordinate to an objective, which it will fail to achieve.

When it measures itself against the *ideal of the ego*, it finds it impossible to agree, to become *one* with the ideal.

The ego usually feels it is up against the impossibility of reaching the perfection posed by the ideal. In the confrontation, it asserts the experience of what it lost when it was no longer "His Majesty, the baby", even though it never had the experience before and never will have it. If it were able to accomplish this unity, it would recover the illusion of uniting with the ideal ego it lost, although in the process it would go out of its mind, which in our practice we call "mania".

However, it is being constantly disturbed by desires not in agreement with the *ideal ego*.

The process of repression which makes us human imposes
on us life in a world ruled by orders, thus leading us to
relentlessly live a history marked by lack

The system of ideals introduced by the humanising process of repression creates an unattainable utopia which humans long for.

We humans, therefore, due to our own psychic condition, will live the *history of a lack*—as Rivera says in the epigraph to this chapter—when facing our system of ideals. We will have to live together with a feeling of insufficiency, of lack in relation to what we would like to be (the perfection of the *ideal ego*) and what we should be (the norms decreed by the *ideal of the ego*).

Repression expels that which conflicts with
human ethical representations

In this process, that which prescribes both what we should be like and what we should not be like yields to repression. This repression appears again in the relationship between the ego and itself. The ego loves that which agrees with the vision it wants to have of itself and hates and rejects that which does not.

We usually assign a protective role to the fulfilment of that which is prescribed by the ideal. Hence, we establish a relationship with the ideal, which is equivalent to the one we have with a belief in somebody or something superior (a belief which neither atheists nor agnostics are usually exempt from). Such a belief gives us an illusory protection in critical situations, in extreme helplessness, when we are haunted by fear, when we are utterly lonely, when we are terrified by the close proximity of death.

The insufficiencies of the ego

Considering the above, the ego, due to its structure, is *an unfortunate beautiful soul* (Hegel, 1807) because its longing for beauty is unattainable.

In the face of the perfections posed by the ideal, the ego always feels an insufficiency it experiences as a handicap or defencelessness; its self-esteem is measured according to the distance the ego feels with regard to that ideal; the relationship between the ego and the ideal allows us to explain the clinical phenomena of both the aesthetic (lovely and ugly) and ethical (good and bad) handicap.

The human ego, due to its origin, is condemned never to attain its own ideal, never to achieve being identical to the ideal image it has of itself, never to match the ideal. The human ego is "becoming" rather than "being", thus, its temporary existence is marked by its non-acceptance of being what it is and by its desire to be what it is not.

Nevertheless, this is not the end of the ego's misfortunes, since the ego does not put up with this essential "lack in being".

The ego, judgement of attribution, and judgement of existence

There are two different versions of what we consider an insufficiency, using the ideal as a reference system: what is considered by judgement of attribution and what is implied by judgement of existence (Figure 7.1).

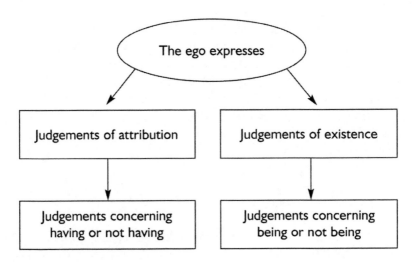

Figure 7.1. The ego's expressions.

The judgement of attribution comprises that which is *unpleasant*, including *guilt*, *disgust*, *shame*, and *fear*, all of them barriers established in the system ruled by the pleasure principle. The judgement of existence comprises that which generates deep existential anguish and it even includes survival: the lack of significance, the destruction of significance, that which will never have significance. The judgement of existence informs the ego about that which is related to horror, to what is ominous, to what is strange. All of these feelings are evidence of processes within the system that is beyond the pleasure principle.

Judgement of attribution

By means of the "judgement of attribution", the ego can judge the attributes it has or does not have and those it does not have and would want to have, as well as those it has and would want not to have.

Among the attributes it would want not to have we should mention those which are the result of having desires it would want not to have, desires which, if it admits it *has*, would make it feel ashamed, desires it should take charge of if repression fails. It is a task of the ego to admit them as its own, be responsible for having them, carry them out, or eventually condemn them.

Judgement of existence

The ego must not only struggle with significances it feels are negative, such as unpleasant ones coming from desires which are disreputable according to its ideals. It must also struggle with things that lack significance. It is not only a question of negative attributes it does not want to have, but of a lack of significance, or of significances that involve it in its ontological essence and, thus, acquire a traumatic dimension.

From this perspective, there is a new negative addition to the negative derived from the judgement of attribution (having or not having). It is the judgement of existence—being or not being. It is added to what brings about guilt or shame in a field familiar to the ego; something which is not fit to be represented, which looks strange, dirty, horrible, or sinister.

Shame and humiliation

I found it necessary to describe this general outlook in order to state that I place the experiences and emotions of shame and humiliation among the misfortunes of the ego. In my opinion, they are feelings that can only be understood in such a context. In other words, it is only in the ego that they may be experienced.

What is more, shame and humiliation are feelings experienced by the ego in reference to its ideals and they are comprehensible only at the heart of the relationships woven by the ego in human connections, both with family and with society.

Shame

Shame does not bring about alterations in the ego at the level of "being": shame is the difficult emotion that is a consequence of the ego's being aware of its inadequacy to the ideal. Such inadequacy is due to the fact that the ego has attributes it would not want to have as a result of desires declared disreputable by the system of ideals.

Shame is a painful sensation felt by the ego as a consequence of having had desires that led it to commit a *faux pas*, or of having done something which compromises its reputation, or of having exposed something it wishes to conceal. Shame is, therefore, the result of a considerable aversion of the ego for itself or for its actions or desires, and the aversion becomes greater when there is a risk of the inadequacy becoming public (Figure 7.2).

Shame comprises a range of emotional states: dishonour, ignominy, affront, public shame as a consequence of abuse, and disgrace due to hateful behaviours.

The attempt to give vent to the fulfilment of unconscious desires that put the ego to shame might result in symptoms, or produce inhibitions developed by the ego so as not to be exposed to the possibility that such shameful desires should be fulfilled.

From this concept, the symptom is the site where the most intimate shameful desires are somehow fulfilled. Thus, repressed unconscious desires are fulfilled surreptitiously. If such desires did not appear in this hidden way, through the symptom, they would put the ego to shame. Symptoms, then, are a kind of deal, a compromise between the disgraceful desire and the internalised values that are set against it.

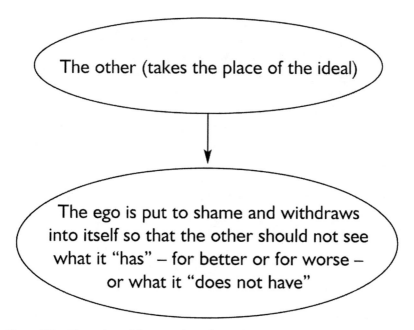

Figure 7.2. The action of the ego when shamed in the eyes of others.

Psychoanalysis proposes that listening to the symptom makes it possible to familiarise the ego with what is shameful and what it would have preferred to ignore or not to admit as its own. Even though symptoms are part of the ego, it does not consider them its own; they are ego-dystonic. It is as if they were imposed on it, since the ego is unable to acknowledge those desires as part of itself without a conflict.

Humiliation

Humiliation refers to a state of disgrace or loss of respect for itself resulting from a wound that has injured the ego, specifically, a narcissistic injury. When I say "narcissistic injury", I refer to an affront the ego is unable to process within the system of the pleasure principle. As I mentioned before, when the ego is able to repress what it dislikes, the result might be a neurotic symptom. Instead, a narcissistic injury shakes up the ego not in the realm of *having*, but in its *being*.

One of the most unbearable affronts to the ego, one that shatters it, is to feel reified. The feeling that usually emerges when the subject is treated like a thing is humiliation. In this case, another person plays a major role, someone who has hurt the pride the subject felt he had, something to which the ego cannot give an answer.

Summing up, in humiliation there is not only a painful distance from the ideal, as happens in shame, but the pain also hurts the ego and questions its essence.

The answer usually offered by the ego in the face of somebody else's show of power, a situation the ego experiences as an attempt on the part of the other to appropriate its self, is called heroic identification.

From this heroic identification, there is an attempt to reverse the situation by trying to destroy the person who caused the humiliation, or to destroy oneself because it is unbearable to live with oneself once one has been humiliated (Figure 7.3).

Alternating between shame and humiliation

We often see cases where there is a passage from shame to humiliation.

When shame cannot be processed by means of repression or inhibition, it sometimes threatens pride. When pride is hurt, it sullies the ego and a feeling of humiliation may emerge (Figure 7.4).

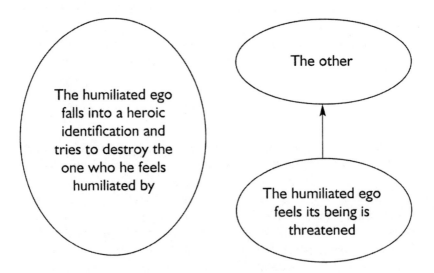

Figure 7.3. Heroic identification when the ego is humiliated.

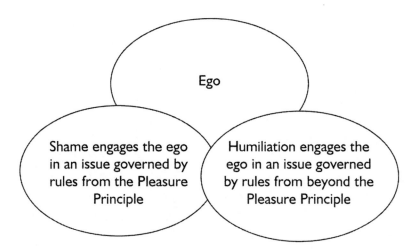

Figure 7.4.   How the ego is engaged by experiences of shame and humiliation.

One often-experienced occurrence begins with humiliation and transits through heroic identification until revenge is exacted against the humiliating agent, which might be the ego itself. The humiliated ego usually rushes into action.

Shame does not necessarily evolve into humiliation; we might feel shame due to an action known only to ourselves because of our own actions or thoughts.

Humiliation and forgiveness

From this point of view, humiliation is closely related to forgiveness. A humiliated person usually feels unworthy of being loved or accepted, or of living a good life because of a past experience, real or imagined. In this respect, forgiving implies a kind of healing of the ego that will allow it not to feel invaded by thoughts or feelings that might drive it to take revenge on those who humiliated it or on itself.

Forgiveness generally requires profound elaboration, since humiliation usually impairs the cognitive capacity needed to assess the complexity of actions and behaviours of oneself and of others. In order to forgive, it is necessary for the ego to suspend causality: in order to forgive we must stop the exasperated search for reasons and causes.

In order to forgive, the one who has been humiliated seeks justice and punishment for the one who has humiliated him. Nevertheless, on occasions, it is not necessary that there should be repentance. Notwithstanding the need for an act of justice, I believe that forgiveness is the result of a process that only takes place within the humiliated person.

Shame and humiliation and the relationship between the individual and the social imaginary

Two notions have been helpful in improving my understanding of the relationship between shame and social values: *social imaginary* (Castoriadis, 1975) and *mentality* (Romero, 1987).

According to Castoriadis (1975), all societies build their own *imaginaries*: institutions, laws, traditions, beliefs, and behaviours. Castoriadis states that the imaginaries are bound to change and that social changes imply essential discontinuities that cannot be explained in terms of deterministic causes or presented as sequences of events.

Romero (1987) defines mentality as the

> set of uses, concrete forms of life, operative ideas which effectively work in a society, which have never been exposed expressly and systematically, which have not been established nor have they ever been part of a pact, but nevertheless feed the system of ideas and rule the system of behaviour of the social group. (p. 140, translated for this edition)

Romero proposes that the mentality of the time plays a major role in the conditions in which a human subject is subjectivised.

In the social imaginary of every society, in each of its historic moments, there emerges what Romero calls a mentality. It is in this framework that I will discuss the issue of how the lack of a feeling of shame, especially when combined with the social imaginary whose mentality justifies its non-existence, gives rise to behaviours that, *a posteriori*, we call "monstrous". The mentality of the time plays a major role in the conditions for the constitution of a human subject, including the conditions under which an act will be considered shameful within the given social imaginary.

Sartre (1952), in his essay on Genet, made an important contribution to the notion of mentality. He believes that for "the *good people*", goodness is equivalent to being, to what already is, and evil is that which questions the "being", the denial, the "not being", the *alterity*. Alterity, for Sartre, is something applied to the being, other than what one really is.

Alterity is, from this perspective, a feeling you have about yourself. The *evil man* would then be a creation of the *good man*, the embodiment of the alterity of what he is, his own negative moment.

For Sartre, evil is a projection. The good man perpetually disowns the negative moment in his actions by means of allowed actions such as keeping, re-establishing, renewing, all of which are repetitive categories, opposed to change. Change causes uneasiness to "*good people*", and uneasiness terrifies them as they do not feel it is a part of them. Faced with the need not to change, "the *good people*" usually accept the values imposed by the prevailing mentality, so they omit the checks to guilt and shame, characteristics of the human order.

In his essay on Genet, Sartre (1952) anticipates the line of thought he will pursue in his *Critique of Dialectical Reason* (Sartre, 1960). In his essay, Sartre conceptualises freedom as the possibility each person has of extricating himself from the conditions in which he has been instituted by society, of the possibility of "departing from the series", of being able to be, to think beyond the limits of the axiological scales which mark the mentality instituted by the social imaginary in different moments of history for how each individual will be and think. Series is a word that in Sartre's works attains the status of a theoretical concept. Series is what makes us be just one more person, no different from the others. "Departing from the series" implies respect for singularity, on the part of oneself and on the part of the social imaginary, which usually punishes those who dare to be different.

A major contribution of psychoanalysis is that its methodology aims to help the patient assume his own singularity without disregarding the awareness that he is, as we all are, a subject of his time. It attempts to create a context where we can subjectively discuss the conflict that usually appears between our particular way of thinking and feeling and the categories with which we were created by society.

In the relationship the individual has with the values set by the society he lives in, especially when this society seems to be "lacking in sense", Arendt (1961) has shaken us with her description of how Adolf Eichmann, in his famous trial in Jerusalem, never showed any signs of remorse or shame for his actions. The analysis proposed by Arendt is an example of the power of the social imaginary, able to rule a mentality (and millions of mentalities) in which that which the human order conceives as shameful becomes part of common sense.

On the complex relationship between shame, humiliation, and forgiveness

What follows are two examples to help illustrate some of the complex relationships between shame, humiliation, and forgiveness, as well as their fluctuations, or, more specifically, the examples demonstrate the different forms assumed by forgiveness, placing emphasis on the role of heroic identification. The first is the narrative of the episode of "Felice" in the Italian film *Tu ridi*,[1] and the second is the novel *Peeling the Onion*, by Günter Grass (2007).

Felice

The first account illustrates the impossibility of processing violence when shame turns into humiliation. The ego can only escape from humiliation or forgive itself by means of a heroic identification, in which it must sacrifice itself to wipe out its humiliation.

Freud (1932a) dealt with the subject of the hero in the myth of Prometheus; Lagache (1951, 1952, 1958), after having made the distinction between the ideal of the ego and the ideal ego, proposes that the latter is the support of heroic identifications. Lagache says that in heroic identification, the ego has the hope of being able to blend with the ideal and is sacrificed in the attempt.

To make it easier for the reader, Felice's story is set indented from the left, in a smaller font, while my comments are set as normal text.

Felice Tespini, the protagonist in the first episode of *Tu ridi*, roars with laughter in his sleep, although he is not a happy man. His wife Marika is angry because she is sure that Felice is making love with some other woman when he is asleep. Felice feels he is being unfairly accused, since he has no memory of the dreams his wife refers to.

Felice feels frustration and failure in his life and thinks he has no valid reason to laugh. He used to be a singer, a baritone, and had to stop singing at the opera because of a heart condition. In addition, he has lost the love of his wife, who had fallen in love with him when he was an opera singer, which he no longer is. His life is dull; his marriage is poor. Ironically, he still works in the theatre, though not on the stage where he had sung in his glory days, but as a clerk. He shares the office with Tobias, a person who must walk with a cane because of a bone defect.

His misfortunes do not end here: one day, on his way to work, he can see a few feet ahead of him that the theatre owner and his two bodyguards are tripping Tobias as he climbs the stairs, making him stumble and fall down. The bodyguards not only laugh, but they heartlessly play with Tobias's cane. Felice is deeply hurt by what happens to his friend and is indignant with those who have ill-treated him. Meanwhile, a friend who is with him joins in the laughter, as if he thought it was just as funny to watch Tobias being ridiculed as the villains did.

Even though Felice is angry at the bullying by the boss and his henchmen and also with the friend who applauds Tobias's stumbling and falling, we cannot see any response on his part to this abuse. Felice seems to be unable to react against the wrongful and abusive power of those who sadistically enjoyed exerting it.

Felice feels he shares Tobias's misfortunes: both are drifting through life with no interest or joy. But it is not only pity and hopelessness which unites them. He is also grateful to his friend for his attention and affection. Strictly speaking, Tobias is the only one who has showed him affection. As a flashback in the story, we see that Tobias had once done Felice's work so that Felice could enjoy the music during a rehearsal at the opera while hiding behind a seat. It is the first time in the film that Felice seems happy. In fact, he had felt so happy at that moment that when the rehearsal finished he could not resist the urge to applaud. However, when the boss, who was also attending the rehearsal, heard the applause, he sent him back to his squalid office.

All through the film, Felice, humiliated, is building a relationship with his boss that is filled with resentment. Time and again, the boss is shown to be a very unpleasant person, arrogant, harsh, a representative of a strict social order, wishing only to command and humiliate.

Felice, worried by the unaccountable night-time laughter which makes Marika so angry, consults a doctor and asks him whether he knows anything about psychiatry. The doctor says he studied the subject at university. Felice tells him about his problem with the laughter. The doctor kindly answers that he laughs because he is dreaming, which Felice promptly denies. The doctor insists that he does dream, but then he cannot remember his dreams, and goes on to add that he laughs because in dreams we all are beautiful souls, like children's souls, and we compensate for our misfortunes with beautiful images which make us happy. Felice does not hesitate to accept this interpretation, though he bitterly regrets his inability to be present at the only place where he can laugh. Later, he feels better by thinking he is "a good man, a beautiful soul".

We see that the doctor's interpretation does not create the conditions for Felice to wonder about his dreams. On the contrary, it works like a dictum when he says that childhood, the stage we return to in our dreams, is the realm of goodness. The good thoughts Felice has in his dreams are a continuation of those he had in his childhood, so it is as if the doctor had said, "There are no evil thoughts in your unconscious."

Both the doctor and Felice, in a narcissistic collusion, reinforce the reciprocity of the illusion that claims "the doctor knows all" and that Felice is not hiding any intention that would mean he is not worthy of God's approval. The doctor and Felice are part of a bond in which there is no need for verifying, thus mutually strengthening the illusion: Felice is not hiding anything, in addition to being good.

Perhaps the doctor is ignorant, but he redeems himself because he does not realise he does not know. He does not like perplexities; he deals with his doubts by means of a knowledge that perhaps is trivial, a common sense that perhaps is uncouth, wrapped in a scientific appraisal. He feels he does not need to investigate either the unconscious or the questions that might arise; this doctor's interpretation does not help Felice to explore what he does not know about himself, his dreams, which are, nevertheless, part of him. Not only that, but the interpretation also disregards the possible existence in his dreams of ideas or desires that might not agree with his "beautiful soul".

When he goes home, Felice tries to convince Marika. He tells her about the doctor's interpretation. Marika does not believe him. That night he laughs in his sleep again, Marika wakes him up and they have a violent argument. So Felice decides to go and sleep in a park. While he is sleeping under a tree, a pine cone falls on his head. For the first time, he is aware of having been dreaming when he wakes up because of the pine cone. And he remembers his dream. In it, he sees the scene he saw at the foot of the stairs when the boss and his henchmen had tripped up Tobias. However, in the oneiric version there are two more elements that did not appear in the original scene witnessed by Felice: Felice, instead of feeling indignant, roars with laughter. He laughs even louder when the hench-men, after playing with the stick, sodomise Tobias with it. Felice, strangely enough, is relieved because he has not been unfaithful to his wife in his dreams.

He runs home to tell Marika that he does not laugh because he is with another woman, but when he gets home he finds that Marika has left him. At that moment, in his empty home, he is frightened to realise that he had been laughing at the fall and the wretchedness of Tobias: in his dream he had been celebrating the tripping of his only friend. He had betrayed him, he had been part of the gang that had humiliated Tobias and had laughed at him.

Felice is ashamed and shocked because of his dream. Soon after this terri-ble insight, he receives the news that his friend Tobias has committed suicide.

Thus, the initial relief because "he is not unfaithful to his wife" in his dreams, does not last long, partly because she has left him, and even more because he has remembered his dream. Before the doctor's words, Felice was just a failure, a man accused by his wife, the only witness to his nocturnal laughter, of a deed he did not believe he had committed. After the interpretation that tells him that while he is asleep he carries out an unconscious action that is essentially harm-less, he is surprised by a dream with a meaning exactly the opposite of what was stated by the interpretation.

When he realises he has been making fun of Tobias's fall, he is aghast. If he accepts the meaning of the dream, it would imply a strong doubt about, or worse, a destruction of, his previous identity as a *good man*, which pits him against a "beyond" that questions his being.

In this state of mind he goes to his friend's wake and promises him (trying to soothe him?) that they will meet again soon. Later, he goes to the opera and overhears the boss muttering to his henchmen that Tobias was an idiot since he could have killed him instead of committing suicide. The boss was sure that Tobias hated him and did not dare to kill him because he was a coward, or, more precisely, an idiot.

Felice feels calm. He feels free of his initial shame and later humiliation. In order to be forgiven, and having heard the boss's words, he decides to avenge his friend. A key condition for that is that he should commit suicide. He writes a note to Marika setting her free to meet a man who can make her laugh.

In his suicidal plan, preceded by the vindication of his friend, he is no longer the unimportant little man he has been up to now, especially after he stopped singing. It is his finest moment. He follows his boss home and makes a noise with the stick while unseen by the boss, pretending to be the ghost of Tobias. The boss is terrified. Felice follows him into the house and threatens him with death. The boss turns into a pathetic man. He is no longer haughty and sure of himself; he is a coward who agrees to write a note admitting his guilt, on condition of staying alive. Once Felice has the note, he leaves and is seen walking, jubilant, towards the sea, where he has chosen to die.

However, something happens that might make him hesitate in his decision. When he arrives at the seaside, Felice meets by chance a woman who is shooting a film there. It is an old love of his, somebody who, years before, had fallen in love with him after she had heard him sing "L'italiana in Algeri". Felice walks with her to a café where they meet the crew working with her. The scene becomes romantic. She urges him to sing an aria from Rossini's opera. Felice hesitates, but then he sings. It seems as if life has smiled upon him again, although in that context in which he seems to become the person he used to be, there is an ominous atmosphere to the film, as if Felice could die while he is singing. When he finishes the aria, he lets the girl go. Nothing will stop him in his inexorable plan, neither the meeting with the attractive and vital woman who fills him with longing nor the pleasure of singing again. The camera focuses on his jacket hanging from a pole on the beach with the note written by the boss inside, and then the lens shifts slowly to the waves, where Felice has been submerged.

The doctor's interpretation did more than fail to open the possibility of representations or emotions that would make questions possible, which would have cast doubt on certainties. It actually closed off such possibilities. It built a narcissistic structure refuting ideas or feelings that might threaten it.

Felice leaves behind his ominous feelings and strengthens himself in a heroic identification, as we will see below. From that place he reverses the situation. He downplays his involvement with those who humiliated Tobias and decides to vindicate him. But in the punishment he wants to inflict on the boss who has tortured Tobias, identifying himself with the pursuer, he finds a breach that includes a punishment for himself.

What is at stake in the vindication is something other than the punishment of the boss for having humiliated Tobias: we must bear in mind that the boss, although he has shown his weakness, remains alive, he is still the boss, he is part of a system against which we can only have moral victories, we can only ridicule him at certain times. In this context, Felice must die to achieve a "moral victory" in which neither he nor Tobias is an "idiot".

A psychopathological digression: if it had only been a question of the guilt of having betrayed a friend, it could have been solved with an obsessive symptom or with a melancholy anticipation that could have led him to self-reproach. But Felice goes one step further. I think that the suicide impulse is the product of an order originating in a heroic identification. Due to this identification, his humiliation causes him to idealise death. Felice is driven to refute his "bad thoughts" and is at the mercy of an order that exceeds his guilt.

As he relies on the heroic identification, his suicide is necessary.

Peeling the Onion

In the account above, we saw that, due to his heroic identification, the only way Felice finds to redeem his friend's dignity and to purge his shame and his guilt for having betrayed him is his own death. For Felice, due to his heroic identification, the boss's note is the only thing that ensures the dignity demanded by this identification. To ensure this dignity, he must die.

To exemplify a different destiny, I will discuss Günter Grass and his novel, *Peeling the Onion*. In the book, Grass wonders, with no self-complacency and with absolute sincerity, about his participation in the SS when he was an adolescent. Here, Grass, who has been an unrelenting judge of the dormant western conscience, is also a judge of himself.

Grass (2007), in his investigation of his own life story, refuses to take refuge in a heroic identification. Instead, he resorts to the person whom he acknowledges as "the most dubious of all witnesses, Mme Memory, a fanciful apparition, often suffering from headaches, and who besides all that, is known to be on sale to the highest bidders" (p. 62). Grass is not deceived by an obliging memory, and time and again he wonders about the young man he once was who joined the Nazi Waffen SS with no compunction at all.

In *Peeling the Onion*, Grass stages a moral drama in which he plays two parts: that of the sinner and that of the redeemer. He both accuses and tries to redeem himself. This duality gives the novel much of its strength, because, in the drama, the author and protagonist does not hide anything and does not conceal himself. Grass speaks his mind, as he has always done, and he believes in the liberating force of his literary work. The product of his inspiration must also serve as a catalyst for his memories.

To assess the effort Grass has made, we must bear in mind that a good number of intellectuals have been harsh judges of the "confession" in his book, reproaching him for not having confessed before.

In the face of this unforgiving criticism, Grass says with great sincerity that he was not aware of the war crimes until the end of the war. *Peeling the Onion*, then, is a drama of memory, slowly developed.

Grass's slow construction acquires a metaphoric value when he seems to be replying to the reader reproaching him for waiting so long to tell his story: it took me a long time too, but for the sake of all onions, I have not concealed anything. See the tears in my eyes! In fact, Grass creates a metaphor where he accuses himself and where, at the same time, he rises above good and evil.

Epilogue

In this chapter, I have proposed that, from my psychoanalytical perspective, the ego's insufficiencies, as well as those denoted and connoted by shame and humiliation, are only conceivable from the references offered by the relationships the ego has with the system of ideals with which it coexists.

Freud (1923b) taught us that the ego represses that which does not agree with its associative and axiological network. Along those lines, the ego frequently not only represses, but also rejects anything that might threaten its coherence or its distance from the ideal. It also usually disowns this rejection.

The violence of the ego, or its reverse, the rushing of the ego into heroic identification, originates in the inevitable insufficiencies the ego presents before the ideal. Additional origins are its difficulty to bear these insufficiencies, as well as the narcissistic injuries that humiliate it for not being able to maintain its fictional unity, its consistent inability to foresee and to predict, and the difficulty in renouncing an ego with a discourse that is both identifying and complete.

I consider it one of the missions of psychoanalysis to provide these irrational feelings with an identity card, these feelings that come into conflict with the tendency of the ego "towards unity and a clear vision" (Camus, 1953). These feelings pose a threat to the ego's longing to become a "beautiful soul" (Hegel, 1807). The ego is annoyed because it is an "unfortunate beautiful soul". Its misfortunes are partly caused by the fact that the ideal, when mentioning all the attributes the ego supposedly had initially, acts as a yardstick for perfection against which the ego always feels it does not measure up.

Summing up, I would say the ego does not like perplexities or surprises and is capable of being cruel. It will insist that *the other is the site of all evils and so if I eliminate the other I will eliminate evil*, either to avoid *the narcissistic injury posed by humiliation*, or to avoid the *obstacle that makes it impossible for it to evade the feeling of shame or the painful sensations of lack in its being*. Moreover, the human ego does not easily accept its failure to understand.

Note

1.   Film shot in Italy in 1999. Directors and screenwriters: Paolo and Vittorio Taviani, based on texts by Luigi Pirandello, Montage: Roberto Perpignani, Music: Nicola Piovani, Photography: Giuseppe Lanci, Stage Design: Gianni Sbarra, Costumes: Mariana Polsky, Actors: Antonio Albanese, Sabrina Ferilli, Luca Zingaretti, Giuseppe Cederna, Elena Ghiaurov, Dario Cantarelli. The script consists of two tragedies, one of which takes place in Rome in the 1930s, the other in Sicily.

CHAPTER EIGHT

Comment V

Carlos Guillermo Bigliani

Rodolfo Moguillansky begins his chapter with a beautiful introduction in which he clearly, cleverly, and didactically summarises the theoretical bases of psychoanalysis. He is especially adept at concepts that are not the easiest to explain and that he later uses to typify humiliation and shame.

Thus, he describes shame as affecting the ego according to the *judgement of attribution* (having or lacking an attribute), an issue he sets "this side of the pleasure principle". For humiliation, in turn, the ego would be affected in its *judgement of existence* (being or not being in a given way), and its conflicts are set "beyond the pleasure principle". In the case of humiliation, the ego would be affected by an affront caused by the power of another (or others) that results in its reification. In both humiliation and shame there is a distance from the ego ideal, although humiliation includes a narcissistic injury of the ego. (I wonder whether there is not a narcissistic injury in both cases.)

Finally, Moguillansky describes how humiliation may plunge the subject into a heroic identification (Lagache) from which an urge arises to destroy the other or his own self (in suicide), though, in the circumstances, *forgiveness* might allow the ego to remain at a distance and to "heal" the experience of humiliation. At the end, he gives us two fine examples of psychoanalysis applied to a film and to a literary work.

In general, I agree with Moguillansky, therefore I will only round out some issues and I will add nuances to the few differences, which mostly are not really differences, but questions I am asking him and myself.

Thus, when quoting Kaës, he remarks on the way repression expels from the conscience that which comes into conflict with its ethical representations. I think it is important to point out that in his initial works, Freud also describes how productions which are not compatible with the conscious system of representation are forced to undergo distorting processes in order to enter the conscience. He describes the mechanisms of oneiric distortion, condensation and displacement, and finally, secondary elaboration.

This last mechanism would give a final "edited version" of the contents of the dream for a better acceptance on the part of "the public"[1] within the conscience.

When all this is not enough, due to repression itself, dreams are forgotten, which gives the name to the first chapter of *The Interpretation of Dreams* (Freud, 1900a). Felice, the protagonist of the film analysed, forgets his dreams and the reason for this forgetfulness is clearly related to their contents.

Moguillansky presents diagrams in which he explains the passage to a heroic identification organised by the ego due to a narcissistic injury produced by humiliation in an attempt to destroy the agent of the injury.

Undoubtedly, this is one of the destinies of humiliation. Among others we might consider the following.

1   An appropriate response from the ego: the subject feels humiliated and reacts with a counter-attack against the offender to a degree that depends on the offence and at the appropriate time in regard to the context. This way of acting presupposes the existence of narcissistic fixations never wholly overcome and accepts the idea that we are all subject to narcissistic suffering.

•   *Sadistic–paranoid outcome*: facing up to the experienced humiliation as seen with a magnifying glass, the subject is engaged in an everlasting vengeful crusade against the object, permanently brooding over the humiliating scene and the project of revenge.

- *Masochistic–melancholy way out*: it takes the classic form of an attack against the object with which the subject identifies himself in his ego; it can evolve as a melancholy self-humiliation (destined to show off the wickedness of the subject with whom he identifies) and might lead to melancholic suicide.
- *Mixed outcome*: in which there are elements contained in the second and third bullet points, above.

I think that the case presented in the chapter, littered with criminals and suicidal wishes (and acts), could fit into the last category. This idea would square with Moguillansky when he points out that from humiliation, "revenge is claimed against the one who has humiliated, who could be one's own ego".

The analysis of Felice's dream might provide us with elements to support this idea. If, as shown by Freud in his analysis of dreams, all the characters in the dream represent the dreamer, Felice's dream would be the expression of both his unacceptable wishes to pursue, scorn, and humiliate his friend Tobias and his wish, fulfilled through his identification with him, to be humiliated in public, thus showing the viciousness of his boss (with whom he is also identified, as we are reminded by Moguillansky when he points out the identification with the pursuer). Here, we see a kind of classic melancholic self-humiliation, as described by Freud in "Mourning and melancholia" (1917e), which, instead of finding its expression by passing on to action (a concrete and public conduct) as would occur in an open case of case melancholy, it can still be partially symbolised in a dream.

In this context, experiences of humiliation and self-humiliation could also be considered within the range of melancholia. This notion allows me to revise the hypothesis proposed by Moguillansky, which maintains that if it were a question of guilt for having betrayed his friend, Felice should resolve his conflicts through an obsessive symptom. Sometimes, in a melancholy-based structure, trivial situations of guilt trigger a regression leading to the dynamics of melancholic suicide. At times, I have the impression that Rodolfo (and myself, in some areas of my work) let our elaborations on humiliation head into the territory of guilt. Thus, in the discussion in the paragraph, "More about forgiveness", Felice's suicidal act would serve to "cleanse shame and guilt". Also, when proposing that Felice's intention is that the boss should "blame himself", would we not be facing this identification, as proposed by Lagache, destined to bring him nearer to the ideal, not to compensate for a feeling of humiliation but of guilt? Felice intends to impose the guilt on the boss, an act that ends up being not enough to moderate his own guilt, which will continue pushing him towards a melancholic suicide.

In any case, I believe it would be helpful to think about normal mourning and the mechanism of detachment (a normal defence mechanism through which the ego manages to distance itself from certain objects, allowing others to be cathexised) in their relationship with forgiveness. Also, melancholic and pathologic frozen mourning can be thought of as similar to, or perhaps an element of, the states of humiliation and heroic identification, as shown in the case of Felice.[2]

As Moguillansky points out, dreams in traumatic neuroses are beyond the pattern of the pleasure principle. But, in Felice's dream, the horrible experience of the protagonist on seeing his friend Tobias as the victim of abuse is not reflected exactly as would happen in a typical dream. There are new elements, which could certainly be attributed to the dynamics of the pleasure principle. One of the new elements is the scene of sodomy. Frosch (1981) describes—in what he calls a paranoid constellation—the way in which an important role is played by the repressed passive wishes, feminine and/or homosexual. He proposes that paranoid patterns may result from present humiliating situations[3] which might reactivate past experiences of child abuse.

Frosch proposes that to the famous proposition "I love him" and all its variants, which, in Freud's classic description, could originate mania, erotomania, jealousy, and megalomania, another variant might be added, that is, "I do not love him (her)—he (she) loves someone else". In this case, homosexuality would be projected and the other would be accused of being homosexual. Thus, he describes what he calls "pimp fantasy" in patients who only attain orgasmic fulfilment as a result of stories of sexual relations (especially homosexual), real or fantasised, told by their partners.

We could hypothesise on the existence of similar repressed passive wishes in humiliation, feminine and/or homosexual, which would also play an important role. This would appear in Felice's dream in the parts which would be under the command of his secret wishes, such as, "I do not love (want to be abused by) my boss; he abuses (loves) Tobias". The arguments in "'A child is being beaten'" Freud

(1919e) about the incestuous meanings of childhood fantasies in which a child is being punished by adults (as happens with Tobias), could reinforce the comprehension of the case and contribute to the construction of the over-determination of Felice's dream. Summing up, it might be understood as a way to express/conceal his repressed wishes of masochistic and homosexual submission to his boss, all of which, as they are unbearable to his conscience, appear to be "suffered" by someone else (Tobias).

In any case, we will never know the real dynamics, since it is very unlikely (fortunately or unfortunately) that Felice will ever associate freely on Moguillansky's couch or mine!

These reflections would also be applicable to the case of young Vinicius, which I present in another chapter of this book and which I feel impelled to reconsider, following these "second thoughts" I have had after commenting on Moguillansky's work.

In relation to the questions our colleague asks regarding forgiveness, it is worth wondering if in order to forgive it is actually necessary "to stop our irritated search for reasons and causes". I personally tend to think that forgiveness may appear at some time during the elaboration of the trauma. This does not necessarily require the interruption of the search—whether irritated, or not—for the reasons and causes which gave rise to the traumatic situation. They may be searched for during a whole lifetime. As Hannah Arendt reminds us, understanding is an endless activity that might not produce final results. With regard to forgiveness, it is important that reasons and causes should be intelligible, since they could also free the victim from his possible fantasies of guilt for having participated in the traumatic situation as an agent (such as the examples of situations of sexual abuse described by Sluzki (1993) in which the victim wonders whether she has provoked the rape). The search for reasons and causes may contribute to the differentiation between forgiveness and denial in the elaboration of a pardon that I conceive as part of a mourning process. This would be the meaning behind Arendt's statement (1992, p. 217) that forgiveness is a "miracle that can be performed by man". She believes that the "*Tout comprendre, c'est tout pardonner*" (Understanding everything means forgiving everything), of general wisdom is wrong. I tend to believe, perhaps siding with the general wisdom in a Freudian way, that conscious comprehension helps in the process. I certainly agree with Arendt that forgiveness is something that suddenly interrupts an automatic process infiltrated by revenge and allows for the appearance of something new. Perhaps, in psychoanalytic terms, we should speak of the interruption of repetitive compulsion.

Afterwards, when he deals with Arendt's analysis of Eichmann, Moguillansky emphasises that during the trial for his foul crimes, Eichmann showed no signs of shame, but only complained because he had wasted his career as an official member of the Third Reich. Of course, this shamelessness is formulated in relation to a moral code which currently exists and which we suppose was absent or was replaced by a different one at a given moment in the life of a certain subject, which might be reinforced, as in this case, by a social imaginary that allows him to agree with that different code. My idea is that shamelessness corresponds to a very intense narcissistic fixation which leads us to ponder the case of Eichmann and similar others (torturers in our Latin American dictatorships, or in the Bush era, as well as undercover police or paramilitary members of extermination groups in all latitudes) as products of the assumption, from the narcissistic structure of these subjects, of prevailing principles in a social imaginary at a given time. These subjects "weld" themselves—uncritically and defensively—into their ideological formation as if it were their mother's body. From this perspective, Eichmann's nostalgic complaint is understandable. It occurred in a final and desperate moment and was aimed at protecting his narcissistic lack of differentiation with his "mother-career" in the Third Reich.

Another interesting point to underline is that the notion of passage between shame and humiliation, guided by the notions of judgement of attribution and of existence, shaped by the dynamics of patterns of within and beyond the pleasure principle, presupposes a conception of the psychic apparatus which authorises the passage from one clinical formation to the other. Lacan, Klein, Freud (to a lesser extent, as he was more sceptical in this respect), and many others acknowledge the possibility of the passage from psychoses to neuroses. But, how would it come about in our own particular case? Would there be a regressive–progressive move? If so, what would it be like, what would make the move impossible, what would happen with the most intense fixations? There are many more questions to pose. We have here an open general field that includes the specific field of humiliation and shame that requires further research. Perhaps Sluzki's chapter in this book would provide an interesting starting point for the research.

I share Moguillansky's literary admiration for Günter Grass, but I am harsher in regard to that chapter of his life. I stand perhaps on the side of his critics. I believe we should revise the idea that Grass "refuses" to take refuge in a heroic identification: the assumption of a heroic identification is inevitable for those who suffer from melancholic dynamics, which includes it. I do not believe this to be the case for Grass. Therefore, it cannot resemble a choice of the ego to refuse or not. I would also tend to revise the idea that in the novel the protagonist does not conceal anything, does not conceal himself, and was "always" outspoken, when what we are dealing with is a belated confession of his collaboration with the Nazis, which he kept concealed for a long time. Probably, as Moguillansky says, "the products of his inspiration must also serve as catalysts for his memories", but I also think we are dealing with "concealing" memories, which Grass poetically admits when he speaks of Mme Memory's frailty. I tend to believe in more intimate confessions (couch confessions?) rather than in public ones that provide millions for authors and publishers.

Nevertheless, I think that this is a good starting point for continuing to think about the important subject of forgiveness. I hope we will meet again to continue with our discussion.

Notes

1. I have frequently used the notion of "the public" within the conscience, especially for readers from different disciplines and young students who need to understand that conscience is "inhabited" by thoughts of others who have left their mark in the ego of the subject, as well as through them, by the culture and the ethics of his time.

2. Ricoeur (1995, p. 80) describes "evasive forgetfulness and liberating oblivion", the latter being associated with the mechanism of forgiveness, which he feels is found at the crossroads of the work of memory and the work of mourning. Ricoeur suggests that forgiveness heals. (The name of the work is: *"Le Pardon, peut-il guerir?"*—Can forgiveness cure?) I believe that cure paves the way to forgiveness.

3. Freud suggests (1911, p. 60) that "a surprisingly important element in the production of paranoia, especially in men, consists of social humiliations and slights".

CHAPTER NINE

Comment VI

Carlos E. Sluzki

I must confess that during the past twenty-odd years I have had few opportunities to read scientific literature that was clearly rooted in psychoanalysis—an intellectual casualty of my dominant interest in the equally vast production in social psychiatry and systemic and social constructionist approaches. None the less, to my surprise, while exploring Moguillansky's chapter, in addition to the aesthetic pleasure provided by being immersed in an intelligent and well-written piece, I experienced a certain nostalgic *saudades* (Ah, the good times of my lost identity as a psychoanalyst! The lost joy, if not the relief, of seeing the world through such an elegant cosmogonic lens!) accompanied, alas, by a sense of distance, of loss of familiarity with that language that, like any other, contains a code that is partly public and partly private, loaded with conceptual echoes known only by those members inducted into and active in the guild.

Perhaps it is due to this distance that, during my first reading of that chapter, I had to struggle (again?) with the recursivity of constructs such as "observing ego" and "observed ego." Among other conundrums, I was puzzled, for instance, by the question "Who observes the observer?" To be more personal: what happens, for instance, during those rare occasions in which I feel myself blushing—

a tell-tale sign of shame—in a social context, while I am unable to uncover what that emotion is about, where it comes from, what scenario awakens it, in spite of my many years of introspection and assiduous occupancy of a psychoanalyst's couch? In other words, I explore my-self (I observe my ego? Or is my ego the one who observes, and in that case, does it observe itself?) but find myself unable to grasp what (unconscious?) rule I have violated by omission or commission in that context. In an effort to make sense of those types of experiences, I had to capitulate and acknowledge the construct of a compartmentalised self that operates with hidden or blocked parts, inaccessible—at least to me!—through introspection but sensitive to context, or even *requiring* context and witnesses. This theme is picked up later below.

The precisions of the English language have certain advantages over the perhaps more literary but certainly more ambiguous Spanish. One such advantage is being able to differentiate—as Moguillansky commented in his fifth endnote, while wisely avoiding taking sides—between "self" as quasi-equivalent to identity and "ego" as a reference to that mediating psychic instance, sometimes accessible to introspection, mediating beyond our awareness between its contentious neighbours, those opposite forces involved in a Titanic struggle in the Valhalla of the unconscious (with apologies for that hybrid metaphor). These are, as the reader well knows, the id, ruled by the pleasure principle and aiming at immediate gratification, blind to any social mandate, and the superego, implacable oppressive principle aimed at controlling and subjugating the savage by whatever means to prevent him from invading and taking over the *homo socialis* of the self.

While powerful in so many aspects, one of the risks that may accompany the use of the construct "ego" is the facility with which it may become reified, and transformed into a sort of homunculus with all the attributes of an individual—the ego suffers, makes efforts, mediates, is relieved—while we therapists de- and re-construct it from outside, collaborating with its tasks the best way we can.

This musing is relevant for the discussion of the preceding chapter, where Moguillansky tends to maintain an appropriately differentiated use of the words *self* (an existential concept) and *ego*, in the psychoanalytic sense. He fuses both versions, however, when he displays one of the central arguments of his core chapter, which is (Felice's) "ego's misfortunes", when the ego discovers the insuperable distance between the protagonist's ideal of perfection and his very imperfect attributes, impulses, and enactments, the homunculus raising its arms in frustration while trying to deal with those looming catastrophic discrepancies.

In his description, Moguillansky displays a healthy empathy with that suffering ego (or is it self?), a necessary stance for carrying out a carefully tuned therapeutic process. Thus, he avoids allying with excessive enthusiasm either with the id's instinctive impulses (imperfect attributes and immediate gratifications strongly criticised during socialisation and severely chastised by all religions) or with the punitive criticisms emanating from the superego (ego ideal that, as with solidarity, is necessary for a life among meaningful others but, as with sanctity, defies any efforts at fully achieving it, regardless of the incentives of a promised eternity in Paradise). It leaves me, none the less, in doubt as to whether we are referring to misfortunes of the ego or of the self.

I wish also to add a nuance to his allusion to "shame about and with oneself", meaning, if I understand it correctly, while in solitude. In my view, that shame is, on most occasions, merely a variation of "shame in social contexts". In fact, one of the social values of shame as a gyroscope that orientates our behaviours is precisely that prospective exploration into hypothetical futures that alerts us to possible embarrassing disasters *vis-à-vis* virtual third parties and allows us to organise alternatives so as to avoid them ("If I did, or did not do, this, I would feel shame."). In addition, it guides us through another equally valuable but more uncomfortable travel through time, the retrospective reconstruction and re-living of an unfortunate public display that has taken place (in front of friendly, neutral, or hostile witnesses) that allows us to re-evaluate it, providing us with the opportunity to try to undo the damage, or at least learn from the experience. ("Now that I realise, I feel so ashamed (*notice the present tense of the verb*) for what I said/did/failed to say/to do.") One way or another, *the witness is a mandatory co-protagonist of any scene and experience of shame and humiliation.*

This discussion about the other's gaze and about the "judgement of attribution" evokes an interesting, while schematic, model of the self proposed years ago by Laing and collaborators (Laing, Phillipson, & Lee, 1966). Written in a tighter language than that mixture of existential psychology and poetry that characterised most of Laing's other writings, the self is described here as composed of (or at least sub-merged into) a "spiral of reciprocal perspectives" that includes my image of you, my image of your image of me, my image of your image of my image of you, and so on *ad infinitum*. The self becomes, in that way, a *collage* that includes view—and judgements—attributed to the Others, intertwined with our image of ourselves and of those Others, whether these are meaningful and specific or generalised. Through that process, the intra- and the interpersonal become indissoluble. At the same time, this model brings forth a terrible existential solitude of our being in this world, of our self, as the Others are defined in large measure as a product of our constructs . . . and vice versa. In fact, this model, and, I should add, much of Fairbairn's exquisite world of projective and introjective identifications, constitutes an interesting prelude to what was developed years later as "social construction-ism". It should not surprise us, then, that self-reflexivity, as well as many mystic views of the cycles of nature and the eternal return, have been symbolised for millennia in many cultures through variations of the *ouroboro*, the snake, or sometimes a dragon, that curves into a circle and bites its own tail.

In both scenarios where shame or humiliation have already taken place or may be predicted, third parties acquire a protagonist's role, as they have the power to amplify or muffle the past or future experience through their own behaviours or by mere attribution of their judge-ment by the main actor. The witness becomes a fair or unfair charac-ter in front of whom the subject becomes ashamed or humiliated. As already discussed in Chapter Four, the capacity of the witness to enhance or reduce the intensity of the experience is contingent on whether he validates the attributed negative judgement—or enacts one—or, on the contrary, displays signs of solidarity or support towards us that define him as a friendly witness. Granted, a good part of the rationale for the psychoanalytical "working through the trans-ference" aims at decontaminating the Other (the psychoanalyst, in this case) from attributions of any kind.

The triadic plot of the narratives of shame and humiliation does not require the active presence of three actors embodying the humili-ated/shamed (self), the humiliator/shamer (other), and the friendly/neutral/hostile witness: that latter role has a ubiquitous attribute that allows it to be lodged in the self (who becomes the humiliated and the humiliator or the shamed and the shaming source), or in the humiliator (who becomes a scornful witness as well), or the third-party witness (who enacts, or is perceived by the humiliated or shamed to be the source of, the critical voice or glance). As discussed on other occasions in reference to political, sexual, and relational violence (Sluzki, 1993), the perpetrator (imagine a torturer or a rapist), frequently adds denigrating comments to his acts, blaming the victim for being the cause of his/her predicament: "You made me do it", in any of its variations, adding complexity to the dynamics of the scene. And, if a person is raised in a blaming, oppressive milieu, the denigrating voice may end up lodged in the victim him- or herself: "I deserve contempt, and the world only confirms that view."

As I discussed in Chapter Four, if we perceive the judgements by (or attributed to) the witness as correct—that is, if we agree with the critical, negative appraisal of self—the dominant emotion will be one of shame and our atavistic reaction will be one of wanting to hide or disappear. ("Swallow me, earth!") Short of exhibiting the raw emotion, an alternative available in certain circumstances and in concert with personal style is to act as if the event/circumstances had *not* taken place, that is, to gloss over, at least in part, the event.[1] Of course, the opposite may be a choice, that is, to display a major apology following a minor transgression, in what ends up becoming a mixture of apology and disqualification of any overreaction by the other.[2] Each of these tacks can be considered parts of a socially and culturally acceptable repertoire of face-saving moves. Exploring the ends of the continuum, at one extreme we find the *seppuku*, or *hara-kiri*, developed originally by the Samurai in Imperial Japan as an honourable reversal of acts considered extremely shameful, such as having an army under their command lose a crucial battle, or being discovered betraying the emperor or the honour code of the caste, or having fallen into the hands of the enemy. In many cases, this self-sacrifice was offered to high-ranking officers in disgrace as a gallant alternative to the less desirable option of being tried and punished or, even worse, being left to live in shame.[3] At the other end of the spectrum can be found the utter indifference to the eyes of the other, examples of which can be found in the anecdotary of kings and emperors of the past, and some that will be mentioned later in this commentary.

In the second scenario, one in which the negative judgement of the co-protagonist/witness is perceived by the subject as *unfair*, either blatantly so, or disproportionately excessive, that is, in the scenario of humiliation, the plot thickens. The display of a negative judgement or a debasing behaviour by a third party presupposes (sometimes establishes) a power relationship between the humiliator/witness and the humiliated where the humiliated subject is at the mercy of the value judgement enacted by, or attributed to, the humiliator, that is, it establishes a higher power position by the latter. The monarch can humiliate a vassal (moreover, he can do it with impunity, and in front of a court of witnesses), the landowner can do it to the indentured peasant, the officer to the soldier, the father to the young son, more easily than the reverse. The vassals, the peasant, the soldier, and the son can only do the reverse if they deny the power or authority of the humiliator (and they are ready to tolerate the potential consequences of that act). Needless to say, and even more if this reversal takes place in front of third parties, either the power is transferred between the actors, or the original perpetrator will in turn be forced to escalate, unleashing terrible consequences towards the one who defied him or her, in order to retain power, thus defining the counter-humiliation as unacceptable.

Moguillansky states in his chapter that to forgive the one who humiliated us and/or to forgive ourselves after being shamed by a behaviour that is later tied to a negative self-judgement helps to heal a narcissistic wound. I do agree with his comments about the process of forgiving. I would like to expand a bit, or perhaps only rephrase, his argument. In essence, the process of forgiveness requires suspension of any effort to reconstruct what Watzlawick, Beavin, and Jackson (1967) named "the punctuation of the sequence of events" (Where and when did this chain of events start? Which is the *true* one to blame, my misstep or the one who laughed about it?) or at least to minimise the distress that is described in his core chapter as an "irritated search". In regard to that issue, this reduction of distress might, in fact, be the result of working through the issues, rather than a prescription aimed at facilitating that process.

In the case of an experience of humiliation, working through it may also require the development of an alternative, equally plausible (for the self) explanation about the inner states or motivations of the humiliator's behaviour ("The other said what he said because of envy, or because he is too competitive, or is a racist, or was having a terrible toothache, or has always been mean . . . and therefore I should not take it personally."). These explanations allow us to contextualise and rationalise, or at least disqualify, those demeaning comments or behaviours as not related to any negative personal attribute of ourselves, but tied to negative traits of the humiliator, or to explanatory mitigating circumstances.

In the case of the experience of shame (in which, I remind the reader, we agree with the other in his/her negative attribution of our trait), the possibility of self-forgiveness requires a relabelling of our behaviours or of the context of the shaming experience as a situation/behaviour that is unusual for us (that is, the exception and not the rule). Or we might consider philosophically that it has the merit of teaching us how to navigate those circumstances in the future, or it may be minimised through one of the many pearls of (perhaps trivial) wisdom of along the lines of "We all have moments of imperfection". If we look at this proposal with a magnifying glass, though, we see it merely as a variation of "Two in distress makes sorrow less".

The reference to "the experience of senselessness that accompanies the traumatic experience" in Moguillansky's core chapter reminded me of the unusually frequent sequence observed as a generative context of post traumatic stress disorder among young soldiers upon return from battlefront experiences, described in the context of the Vietnam War as well as the more recent invasion of Iraq and Afghanistan.[4] The sequence contains the following elements: (a) the development of a strong *esprit de corps* between soldiers within the platoon, a small "band of brothers" (homage be paid to Shakespeare's *Henry V*) whose survival depends on their collective alertness and solidarity, a group loyalty strongly reinforced during their training and essential due to the random violence of being part of an occupying army surrounded by local enemies; (b) a foolish decision made by an officer that exposes members of the platoon to an unnecessarily high risk, such as sending a couple of soldiers on a quasi-suicidal scouting mission into known hostile territory, or even the realisation by a soldier that he has been duped into believing that theirs was a war of liberation while those being liberated consider them invading enemies; (c) the death of one or more of the members of the primary attachment group in that suicide mission or in a surprise attack by the enemy; (d) the iterated message from the commanding structures along the lines of "Don't get sad, get mad", which recommends funnelling stress through violent actions; and (e) the commission of indiscriminate acts of savagery enacted as a revenge for that loss, such as shooting passing peasants, or raping and killing native women (echoes of Mai Lai during the Vietnam war); (f) upon returning to a safe place, or after being discharged, sometimes even without recalling the event in detail, symptoms of PTSD begin to seep in.

As we can see, the scenario entails a very tragic existential trap: an average young man, socialised in the daily "living and letting live", is placed into very abnormal circumstances, forced to follow orders that place him at risk and also organise his emotions, in an altered state of consciousness (characteristic of extreme situations), becomes witness or protagonist of savage acts against innocent human beings that, once out of those consciousness-altering states, cannot be rationalised or owned.[5]

In fact, an interesting contrast can be made between the PTSD spectrum of reactions and the social blindness or utter lack of feelings of empathy towards other human beings that Arendt described in Eichmann during his Jerusalem trial and to which she referred as "the banality of evil" (Arendt, 1964). From this perspective, the PTSD syndrome (in itself a controversial diagnostic entity) can be seen as the triumph of morality, and a proof of how difficult it is for the self to disassociate and generate two disconnected selves, each ruled by a different morality. However, this disassociation appears full force in some young people who have been subjected to repeated acts of cruelty and extreme abuse since childhood. It has also been noted in survivors of extermination camps at the end of the most extreme morally and socially dislocating experience of the past century, the Holocaust, where the basic tenets of living in society deteriorated into a living nightmare. Those who survived the transportation, for days without food or water, the selection for immediate death in the extermination camps, the mass killing and, as an alternative, the famine and many other daily acts of extreme cruelty, were people who, until a few months previously, were responsible citizens who had taken good care of their family, treated their neighbours with courtesy, and participated in cultural activities in their community. They were now transformed into beings capable of stealing a slice of stale bread from the hands of another prisoner, moribund and without the strength to defend it, and eating it in hiding with savage delight, not even registering the ashes that fell around them dispersed by the chimneys of the crematoria, informing them of their own imminent destiny. Interviews conducted with survivors of concentration/extermination camps ("the living dead", as they were named by their liberators because of their spectral looks and behaviour), frequently show this phenomenon of the split or double self. These are people who were rescued, physically cared for upon liberation, occasionally reunited with a surviving family member, and who, upon emigrating to another country, who re-built a solid persona, as well as a responsible personal and professional life and frequently a new family, subjects they discuss comfortably. But when they are invited to talk about their past ordeals and they choose to do so, almost instantaneously their physiognomy, voice, and gestures change while they describe, in an indifferent voice and frequently using present tense verbs, the most horrendous experiences, drastically discontinuous from the current reality and morality. Langer, in his extraordinary book, *Holocaust Testimonies: The Ruins of Memory* (Langer, 1999), describes that process as the emergence of a disassociated self, an extreme way of dealing with experiences of horror, humiliation, shame, and daily suffering so profoundly dislocated from their current self that they cannot share the subjective territory of the same *homo socialis*. This dissociation allows for the framing of these two realities as two discontinuous worlds, avoiding moral judgements and overwhelming experiences of shame and humiliation that would be devastating should the two selves merge into one.[6]

To shift to a different topic, Moguillansky's speculation about the origins of one of his key character's negative traits evokes the old question: How much of a *tabula rasa* is the newborn? I wish to offer some extended commentary on the subject.

Nowadays there is little doubt about the complex interaction in a person's makeup between genetic proclivities (what is conveyed by the genome as potential and as dominant style), what is expected by the parents (what is desired, feared, and, in one way or another, projected and enacted by them on the infant), and the cultural mandates transmitted and modelled by the social world that surrounds the infant. (See, on this subject, crucial contributions by Fivaz-Dupeursinge and Corboz-Warnery, 1999; Reiss, Plomin, Neiderhiser, & Heathrington, 2003; and my own musings, Sluzki, 2006.) In this regard, an exemplary research project carried out by the team under the leadership of Wynne and Tienari merits being highlighted (Tienari, Wynne, & Wahlberg, 2006; Tienari et al., 1994, 2004; Wahlberg et al., 2004; Wynne et al., 2006a,b, as well as the extensive review of this longitudinal research project in Sluzki, 2007). This project entailed the long-term follow-up of two matched samples of infants: one whose mothers had been diagnosed with schizophrenia prior to the delivery, and another whose mothers had not received any psychopathological diagnosis. All of them were given up for adoption, without labelling their family history, to "normal" families (defined by the social service agencies in charge of adoption processes as competent and without any psychiatric history). Considering that, statistically, the probability of manifestation of schizophrenia in offspring of a parent with that diagnosis is ten times higher than that of the general population, the infants of the first sample were labelled as "high risk" and those of the second sample as "low risk". The adoptive families, children included, were interviewed at different points throughout the following twenty years and classified, following operationalised criteria, in regard to interpersonal, structural, and communicational traits, into three groups: highly functional, average functional, and low functional. The latter applied to either extremely rigid or extremely chaotic families. Twenty years after adoption, the cluster with a combination of "high risk" adoptive child and low functioning family displayed all the expressions of severe psychopathology in the adopted child, followed by the combination "low risk" child and low functioning family. In contrast, none of either high- or low-risk children adopted into highly functional families showed any psychopathological traits.

In sum, there is little doubt that, far from being a *tabula rasa*, newborns bring with them proclivities and styles that interact with their parents' styles and resulting interactive patterns—affected, of course, by other multiple other variables of their surrounding milieu—that contribute to organising their experiential world. These variables include a greater or lesser contribution of guiding social emotions, some positive ones such as joy, reaffirmation, and eudemonia, some "negative" (corrective) ones such as those we have been discussing in this book.

In closing, I wish to propose an alternative, less critical reading of a component of the film plot that occupies part of the second section of Chapter Seven, that is, Moguillansky's comments about the "interpretation" proposed by Felice's physician for his patient's dreams, or lack of them. As we may recall, Felice was extremely distressed by his own intriguing laughter while asleep, which his wife found irritating, and filled him with guilt (an emotion triggered by his wife's nagging complaints, as he himself does not remember any content when he wakes up, even though, in itself, that may hint of "forbidden" dreams). The physician told Felipe that, while he might not remember his dreams' content, he shouldn't worry, as dreams are populated by beautiful souls, as if children's dreams. He added that joyful dreams are ways in which we compensate for the unhappiness of real life. Until that moment, Felice was not only accused by his wife for having imaginary transgressions (poor woman, emotionally deprived and barren of love, resentful just because her husband seemed to be having a good time in dreamland, while she didn't seem to be able to do so either asleep or awake!), he was also feeling guilty about betraying his wife just by laughing. In his comment, the physician labels dreams, repressed dreams included, as good and innocent, taking place in a limbo where sin does not exist.

In my view, far from being a narcissistic collusion or an act of professional incompetence, the physician's comments constitute a lucid positive connotation, as he manages to shift the sign of Felice's "symptom" from negative to positive, giving him permission to dream in peace. It may even be an authorisation for some of his dream's content to emerge into consciousness; a risky mixed blessing in this case. If there is a criticism that can be made of the physician, it is that he let Felice go without establishing the continuity of a therapeutic process. This lack of follow-up plans transforms his wise reframing of the dream into a "wild interpretation" without subsequent restraint about its potential effects. As we well know, these could be either a blessing or a chain effect of unpredictable outcomes (in this plot, a tragic one). In my view, a large part of the denouement of the story derives from the fact that Felice's wife, on whom he is dependent and quite regressively attached, abandons him. He is humiliated once again, this time with an unannounced act of contempt, which defines him as incompetent, impotent, forsakable. The two lines of the plot intertwine here: he has been a coward in both scenarios—with his friend and with his wife—and he has no other choice but to redeem himself in order to close the story: to live in peace, but without a job? Without this nagging woman to whom he is so attached? Or to die in peace, crowned by a final self-punishment to pay for his double shame of not having confronted the aggressors, real and imagined, of the people he loved, his friend and his wife. In sum, the physician's intervention, while insufficient in terms of lack of containment and continuity, is extremely felicitous: "Do not be afraid of your dreams, they are transparent in their symbolism, like those of children."

In closing, and returning to a statement I made at the beginning of my commentary, the elegance with which Moguillansky conveys his views in the previous chapter generates a text that is aesthetically and conceptually rich, allowing the reader to think as well as to resonate emotionally, to learn while enjoying the process. I hope that my comments add some nuances to his text without disturbing its overall effect.

Notes

1. A colleague told me of a situation in which she was ushering a family into her office for a weekly therapy session when a sanitary pad she was wearing fell out, bloody surface upward, practically in the middle of room, in plain view of the family. They proceeded to sit down without any comment, displaying gracious social ignorance. Blushing ferociously, she managed to mumble, "Excuse me for a minute," picked up the pad with two fingers and left the room. She went into the restroom to dispose of the pad and attach (this time securely!) another one, and did the best she could to calm herself down. Then, struggling against her desire to suspend the session, cancel her practice, and leave the country for parts unknown, she returned to the office, commenting in a low voice "How embarrassing!", the adults responding with tender smiles denoting sympathy, and went on with the consultation—to the relief of the family, who, in the meanwhile, appeared to have remained in tense silence, the children giggling and the parents looking at them sternly. Needless to say, that episode was never mentioned again throughout that therapy, the therapist oscillating between relief and a sense that somehow she should explicitly bring the issue out and rob it of some of its power as a shaming memory by trivialising it.
2. Such as a major florid apology after having sneezed or coughed discretely in the course of an informal interaction, as if those reflexes were not autonomous and beyond our control.
3. In fact, this tradition remains alive in Japan if one considers the high incidence of suicide among CEOs of high-ranking enterprises following an entrepreneurial debacle.
4. Unfortunately, I have not been able to pinpoint the original source of this

observation. However, I can confirm it through my own clinical experience with a number of symptomatic patients who had been exposed to those unfortunate contexts.

5.   The possibility of working through and reconciling with the barbaric acts carried out by individuals during war is dramatically reduced when the soldiers, upon returning to their own country, are confronted with a critical, hostile public opinion about that very war and, by extension, about their own prior ordeal. That was the case of the soldiers returning from Vietnam and, in general terms, soldiers from a defeated army. The current prohibition against filming any live military action carried out by the USA's armed forces is clearly intended to avoid exposing Americans to the naked brutality of an armed intervention (that, taking place abroad, can be comfortably forgotten) and so avoid the negative public opinion that those televised images generated during the Vietnam confrontation.

6.   People emerging from extreme situations call into question the universality of the mandate of orientating our therapeutic work with traumatised patients towards the integration of disassociated components of the self: perhaps these extreme disassociations are necessary for their survival, or at least for a modicum of sanity. However, the opposite is true for the collective conscience: the disassociation of terrible collective memories risks their being forgotten. As has been repeated many times in quotes and paraphrases, those who forget the past are at risk of repeating it (Santayana, 1905, as an aphorism, and Freud, not much later and in a much more sophisticated fashion in his description of repression as well as of repetition compulsion (Freud, 1915d and 1920g, respectively).)

Epilogue

Carlos Guillermo Bigliani, Rodolfo Moguillansky,
and Carlos E. Sluzki

T he two Voyager space probes, launched in 1977, have been continually propelled along in their trajectory by the gravitational pull of the planets of the solar system. Not only do they offer a completely new vision of our planets, with their extraordinary photographs and endless surprises, they are continuing their voyage towards interstellar space, and have already reached a distance of sixteen million kilometres from the sun. There is hope that they may be detected by some intelligent species living in those parts of the universe crossed by their path, no one knows how many thousands of years from now, or what those species will be like. These probes carry with them keys that aim to explain where they are from in the universe, which are the morphological and paradigmatic characteristics of the senders.

In a shamelessly pompous comparison, when we started on our adventure that led to the meeting that in turn resulted in this book, our expectations were to present to each other, and to a public, the characteristics of our respective points of view, our keys, and to attempt to discuss them from each other's conceptual perspective. We did not have a very clear idea, however, of the nature of the ideological species we would find in each other's reasoning during that process.

We knew from the start that the directions of our referential paths were divergent: some of our personal conceptual probes had as a starting point an intrapsychic base while exploring the interpersonal space, while others had as point of departure the world of relationships and only occasionally would impinge on the intrapersonal realm. In the course of our exchanges, these trajectories were occasionally corrected and adjusted, sometimes thanks to the gravitational force of arguments emanating from intrapsychic or interactional constructs, sometimes due simply to the turbulences generated by the crossing of each other's trajectory in conversation.

However, with the exception of some differences in language and referents, our dialogues have been surprisingly easy, or at least fluid: rather than an encounter with alien species, we shared many elements of culture, history, and training, and, why not, personal style, that added substantial familiarity with one another's parameters, and ways of presenting and applying them.

It should be acknowledged that the three of us were aware that, if we settled our optic only within our private omni-explanatory cosmogony (and both the psychoanalytic and the systemic paradigms can foster that call for exclusivity), the whole of reality would be tinged by that perspective and we would end up relating to our model as a theology full of revealed truths, while considering the other as a lost soul with no knowledge or desire to be blessed by our enlightenment. For that reason, we did our best not to fall into sectarianism, struggling against the secret temptation to take for granted that "my model is the best" and favouring a good willing search for conceptual resonances, which increased not only our sensibility, but also our sympathy towards what the others were saying. We were, in fact, following the implicit advice contained in one of Freud's letters to Lou Andreas-Salomé dated 7 July 1914 (Pfeiffer, 1985): "I never struggled against differences of opinions within Psy research, mainly because I usually have more than one opinion about each problem".

And so it happened, if we may drastically change metaphors midway (while seemingly unable to relinquish their grandiosity!), that the encounter of the tectonic plates of our models did not generate any of the earthquakes that we predicted (or hoped?) may have taken place. At the most there were some minor tremors, but, alas, no major catastrophes.

Moreover, our position concerning debate has been that the inter-personal and intrapersonal models, even though they are cosmogonic in respect of many of their issues, can extend out far enough to allow the development of conceptual bridges in their intersections. From the psychoanalytic point of view, notions such as projective identification extend the self beyond the individual in order to include the other to configure what Laing, a highly heterodox psychiatrist with some psychoanalytical and a lot of existential training, and his colleagues (Laing, Phillipson, & Lee, 1966) called "the spiral of reciprocal pers-pectives" (my image of you, my image of your image of me, my image of your image of my image of you, and so on) as one of the bases of the self-in-a-relational-world . . . and a source of many interpersonal misunderstandings. From a systemic point of view, in turn, it is worth remembering that one of its most resonant preludes, the "double bind" theory about the interpersonal contribution to the causation of schizophrenia (Bateson, Jackson, Haley, & Weakland, 1956), was described as taking place both in the interpersonal world and in the introjects of the individual (although those authors were using a different terminology). Furthermore, one of the institutions that was crucial in the development of family therapy, a practice that is essen-tially relational, was founded in New York by an iconoclastic psycho-analyst, Nathan W. Ackerman, who moved freely across the border between the relational and the intrapsychic world. In fact, one of the earliest training films in the field of family therapy—the so called Hillcrest Family Interviews—allows us to witness Ackerman conduct-ing a conjoint interview with a family of five in which he interprets the Oedipal fantasies of one of this family's young sons while explor-ing collective interactional patterns.

However, there have been a number of therapists with a psycho-analytic background who established clear-cut boundaries between paradigms. That is the case, for instance, of the well-known Italian psychoanalyst, Mara Selvini Palazzoli. Her team, an extremely crea-tive and influential quartet that contributed substantially to the devel-opment of systemic models, had as a norm, when they began their exploration of interactional processes and their treatment of families with severe pathology, to avoid any psychoanalytical reference while discussing them, in order to be able to explore the power of the models proposed by Gregory Bateson and the Mental Research Insti-tute researchers and therapists that followed him (see, for example,

Selvini Palazzoli, Boscolo, Cecchin, & Prata, 1974). They, as well as many others, considered intra- and interpersonal epistemologies to be discontinuous, and they treated them as such.

It is not excessively difficult, indeed, to find bridges or to find chasms when we devote ourselves to seek areas of possible harmony or of possible incompatibility: to a great extent we may find what we are looking for. We have chosen to find, or build, some bridges at the expense of diminishing the possible earth-shaking (though sometimes attractive) intensity of confrontational debates. In sum, we opted for an open and amiable discussion, using as our conceptual overarching background a social constructionist extension of Bertrand Russell's (1914) formulation about "theories being merely symbolically constructed fictions".

We know very well that we do not provide a closure for the reader, that our conceptual trajectories have not melted into a happy marriage, that the dialogue remains open. In fact, we hope to have facilitated the incursion of the readers into the issues under discussion without having forced them to take sides, although perhaps without solving for them some conceptual riddles and questions. Still, questions are the fuel that keeps alive the fire of the scientific enquiry into these and so many other models. They help us to verify or falsify models as well as to explore their boundaries and grey zones, adding new points of view, exploring new practices, and examining them to find in turn the emergence of new questions, *ad infinitum*. We hope that a couple of those steps will have taken place while reading this book.

REFERENCES

Aberastury, A., & Knobel, M. (1984). *La Adolescencia Normal*. Buenos Aires: Paidós.

Abraham, N., & Torok, M. (1978). *L'ecorce et le noyau* [The Shell and the Kernel]. Paris: Aubier Flamarion.

Achenbach, T. M. (1978). The child behavior profile: I Boys aged 6–11. *Journal of Consulting and Clinical Psychology, 46*: 478–488.

Ackerman, N. (1958). *The Psychodynamics of Family Life*. New York, Basic Books.

Alexander, A., & French, T. M. (1946). *Psychoanalytic therapy: Principles and Application*. New York: Ronald Press.

Anzieu, D., & Martin, J.-Y. (1965). *La dynamique des groupes restreints* [Dynamics of Small Groups]. Paris: PUF.

Appignanesi, L., & Forrester, J. (1992). *Freud's Women*. London: Weidenfeld and Nicolson.

Arendt, H. (1951). *The Origins of Totalitarianism*. Cleveland, OH: Harcourt, Brace, Jovanovich.

Arendt, H. (1961). *Eichmann in Jerusalem: A Study on the Banality of Evil*. New York: Penguin, 1994.

Arendt, H. (1992). *Between the Past and the Future*. New York: Penguin.

Aulagnier, P. (1975). *The Violence of the Interpretation*. New York: Routledge.

Aulagnier, P. (1984). *The Apprentice Historian and Master Sorcerer*. Paris: PUF.

Basak, J. (2009). Una perspective psicoanalítica de la "Prohibición de no mirar" japonesa—Japón e India [A psychoanalytic perspective of the Japanese "prohibition against looking"—Japan and India]. *Revista de APDEBA, XXXI*(2/3): 269–284.

Bateson, G. (1972). *Steps to an Ecology of Mind: Collected Essays in Anthropology, Psychiatry, Evolution, and Epistemology*. Chicago, IL: University of Chicago Press.

Bateson, G., Jackson, D., Haley, J., & Weakland, J. (1956). Toward a theory of schizophrenia. *Behavioral Sciences, 1*(4): 251–264.

Baumeister, R. F., Stillwell, A., & Wotman, S. R. (1990). Victim and perpetrator accounts of interpersonal conflicts: autobiographical narratives about anger. *Journal of Personality & Social Psychology, 59*(5): 994–1005.

Benedict, R. (1946). *The Chrysanthemum and the Sword: Patterns of Japanese Culture*. Boston, MA: Houghton Mifflin.

Berenstein, I. (1976). *Familia y enfermedad mental* [Family and Mental Illness]. Buenos Aires: Paidos.

Berenstein, I. (1981). *Psicoanálisis de la estructura familiar* [Psychoanalysis of Familiar Structure]. Buenos Aires: Paidos.

Berenstein, I. (2004). *Devenir otro con los otro(s): Ajenidad, presencia, interferencia* [Becoming one with the others: Alterity, presence, interference]. Buenos Aires: Paidos.

Berenstein, I. (2007). *Del ser al hacer* [From Being to Doing]. Buenos Aires: Paidos.

Bigliani, C. G. (2003). Os analistas da diáspora [Analysts in the diáspora]. In: M. O. F. França (Ed.), *Freud, a cultura judaica e a modernidade* (pp. 171–190). São Paulo: Editora Senac.

Bigliani, C. G. (2009). Projeto terapêutico, Percurso [Therapeutic project and process]. *Revista de Psicanálise, XXII*(43): 163–166.

Bigliani, C. G., & Dines, A. (2001). Unpublished presentation at the exhibition "Freud and Judaism". Club Hebraica, São Paulo, Brazil.

Bion, W. R. (1958). *Experiences in Groups*. London, Tavistock.

Bion, W. R. (1962). *Learning from Experience*. London, Tavistock.

Blum, H. P. (1994). The confusion of tongues and the psychic trauma. *International Journal of Psychoanalysis, 75*(5/6): 871–882.

Borges, J. L. (1960). *The Aleph and Other Stories*. London: Penguin, 2000.

Boszormenyi-Nagy, I., & Framo, J. L. (1965). *Intensive Family Therapy*. New York: Harper and Row.

Buchbinder, E., & Eisikovitz, Z. (2003). Battered women's entrapment in shame: a phenomenological study. *American Journal of Orthopsychiatry, 73*: 355–366.

Buss, A. H., & Plomin, R. (1984). *Temperament: Early Developing Personality Traits*. Hillsdale, NJ: Lawrence Erlbaum.

Camus, A. (1953). *The Myth of Sisyphus*. New York, Vintage, 1991.

Caspi, A., Elder, G. H., & Bem, D. J. (1987). Moving against the world: life course patterns of explosive children. *Developmental Psychology, 23*: 308–313.

Caspi, A., Elder, G. H., & Bem, D. J. (1988). Moving away from the world: life course patterns of shy children. *Developmental Psychology, 24*(6): 824–831.

Castoriadis, C. (1975). *The Imaginary Institution of Society*. Cambridge, MA: MIT Press.

Cienfuegos, A. J., & Monelli, C. (1983). The testimony of political repression as a therapeutic instrument. *American Journal of Orthopsychiatry, 53*(1): 43–51.

Claus, H. (1978). *The Desire*. London: Penguin.

Cobb, S. (2004). Fostering coexistence in identity-based conflicts: towards a narrative approach. In: A. Chayes & M. Minow (Eds.), *Imagine Coexistence* (pp. 294–310). San Francisco, CA: Jossey Bass.

Conran, M. (1993). Algunas consideraciones sobre la vergüenza, la culpa y el perdón, principalmente basadas en El Rey Lear [Some considerations on shame, fault and pardon, mainly based on King Lear]. *Rev. De Psicoanálisis, 50*(4/5): 839–857.

Conway, C. A., Jones, B. C., Debruine, L. M., Little, A. C., Hay, L., Welling, L. L. M., Perrett, D. I., & Feinberg, D. R. (2008). Integrating physical and social cues when forming face preferences: differences among low and high-anxiety individuals. *Social Neuroscience, 3*(1): 89–95.

Dennissen, J. J. A., Asendorpf, J. B., & van Aken, M. A. G. (2008). Childhood personality predicts long-term trajectories of shyness and aggressiveness in the context of demographic transitions in emerging adulthood. *Journal of Personality, 76*: 67–99.

Dershowitz, A. M. (1994). *The Abuse Excuse: and other Cop-outs, Sob Stories, and Evasions of Responsibility*. Boston, MA: Little, Brown.

Dicks, H. (1970). *Marital Tensions*. London: Karnac, 1994.

Eiguer, A. (1983). *Un divan pour la famille* [A Couch for the Family]. Paris: Le Centurión.

Eisenberg, N., Cumberland, A., Spinrad, T. L., Fabes, R. A., Shepard, S., Reiser, A., Murphy, B. C., Losoya, S. H., & Guthrie, I. K. (2001). The relation of regulation and emotionality to children's externalizing and internalizing problem behavior. *Child Development, 72*: 1112–1134.

Enríquez, M. (1996). El delirio en herencia [The delusional inheritance]. In: R. Kaes, H. Faimberg, M. Enriquez, & J. J. Baranes (Eds.), *La transmisión de la vida psíquica entre generaciones* [The transmission of psychic life across generations] (pp. 97–129). Buenos Aires: Amorrortu.

Enríquez, E. (1999). *Da horda au estado: Psicanalise do vínculo social* [From the Horde to the State: Psychonalaysis of the Social Bond]. Rio de Janeiro: Jorge Zahar.

Faimberg, H. (1988). The telescoping of generations: genealogy of certain identifications. *Contemporary Psychoanalysis, 24*: 99–111.

Ferrater Mora, J. (1979). *Diccionario de filosofía*. Madrid: Alianza, 1984.

Ferreira, A. J. (1966). Family myths. *Psychiatric Research Report, 20*: 75–90.

Feyerabend, P. K. (1970). *Problems of Empirism*. Oxford: Cambridge University Press.

Feyerabend, P. K. (1999). *For and Against the Method*. Chicago, IL: University of Chicago Press.

Fivaz-Dupeursinge, E., & Corboz-Warnery, A. (1999). *The Primary Triangle: A Developmental Systems View of Mothers, Fathers and Infants*. New York: Basic Books.

Freud, S. (with Breuer, J.) (1895d). *Studies on Hysteria. S.E., 2*. London: Hogarth.

Freud, S. (1896). Further remarks on the neuro-psychoses of defence. *S.E., 3*: 162–186. London: Hogarth.

Freud, S. (1900a). *The Interpretation of Dreams. S.E., 4–5*. London: Hogarth.

Freud, S. (1905d). *Three Essays on the Theory of Sexuality. S.E., 7*: 125–245 London: Hogarth.

Freud, S. (1909b). *Analysis of a Phobia in a Five-year-old Boy. S.E., 10*: 3–149. London: Hogarth.

Freud, S. (1911c). *Psycho-analytic Notes on an Autobiographical Account of a Case of Paranoia* (Dementia Paranoides). *S.E., 12*: 153–249. London: Hogarth.

Freud, S. (1914c). On narcissism: an introduction. *S.E., 14*: 73–102. t. London: Hogarth.

Freud, S. (1915d). Repression. *S.E., 14*: 143–158. London: Hogarth

Freud, S. (1916–1917). *Introductory Lectures on Psycho-Analysis. S.E., 15*. London: Hogarth.

Freud, S. (1917e). Mourning and melancholia. *S.E., 14*: 239–258. London: Hogarth.

Freud, S. (1919e). 'A child is being beaten'. A contribution to the study of the origin of sexual perversions. *S.E., 17*: 179–204. London: Hogarth.

Freud, S. (1920g). *Beyond the Pleasure Principle. S.E., 18*: 7–64. London: Hogarth.

Freud, S. (1923b). *The Ego and the Id. S.E., 19*: 3–66. London: Hogarth.

Freud, S. (1926d). *Inhibitions, Symptoms and Anxiety. S.E.*, 20: 77–174. London: Hogarth.

Freud, S. (1932a). The acquisition and control of fire. *S.E.*, 22: 187–194. London: Hogarth.

Freud, S. (1933b). Why war? *S.E.*, 22: 197–215. London: Hogarth.

Freud, S. (1939a). *Moses and Monotheism. S.E.*, 23: 3–137. London: Hogarth.

Freud, S. (1940e[1938]). Splitting of the ego in the process of defence. *S.E.*, 23: London: Hogarth.

Freud, S. (1950). Extracts from the Fliess papers. *S.E.*, 1: 177–279. London: Hogarth.

Friedman, L. (1999). *Identity's Architect: A Biography of Erik H. Erikson.* London: Free Association Books

Frosch, J. (1981). The role of unconscious homosexuality in the paranoid constellation. *Psychoanalytic Quarterly*, 50: 587–613.

Gadamer, G. (1975). *Truth and Method.* London: Sheed and Ward.

Goethe, J. W. (1828–1829). *Faust: A Tragedy.* New York: W. W. Norton. 2000.

Goldsmith, H. H. (2003). Genetics of emotional development. In: R. Davidson, J. K. R. Scherer, & H. H. Goldsmith (Eds.), *Handbook of Affective Sciences* (pp. 295–319). London: Oxford University Press.

Grass, G. (2007). *Peeling the Onion.* New York, Harcourt.

Gray, J. (2007). *Black Mass: Apocalyptic Religion and the Death of Utopia.* New York: Farrar, Straus & Giroux.

Green, A. (2004). Enigmas de la culpa, misterio de la vergüenza [Enigmas of blame, mystery of shame]. *Rev. Chilena de psicoanálisis*, 21(1): 58–67.

Gribinski, M. (1994). The stranger in the house. *International Journal of Psychoanalysis*, 75: 1011–1021.

Grinberg, L. (1964). Two kinds of guilt: their relation with normal and pathological aspects of mourning. *International Journal of Psycho-analysis*, 45: 366–371.

Haley, J. (1969). *The Power Tactics of Jesus Christ and Other Essays.* New York: Avon Books.

Harper, J. M., & Hoopes, M. H. (1990). *Uncovering Shame: An Approach Integrating Individuals and their Family System.* New York: Norton.

Hawthorne, N. (1850). *The Scarlet Letter.* Boston, MA: Tickson, Reed & Fields.

Hayner, P. B. (2002). *Unspeakable Truths: Facing the Challenges of Truth Commissions.* New York: Routledge.

Hegel, G. (1807). *Phenomenology of Spirit.* Cambridge: Oxford University Press, 2004.

Heloani, R., & Barreto, M. (2008). *Assedio moral no trabalho.* São Paulo: Ed. Cengage.

Hornstein, L. (2008). *Proyecto terapéutico de Piera Aulagnier al Psicoanalisis Actual* [Psychonalaytic Project of Piera Aulanger to Current Psychoanalysis. Buenos Aires: Paidos.

Ikegami, E. (2003). Shame and the Samurai: institutions, trustworthiness and autonomy in the elite honor culture. *Social Research, 70*(4): 1351–1378.

Jones, E. (1957). *The Life and Work of Sigmund Freud.* London: Hogarth Press.

Jorge, L. (2008). Interview. Accessed at: www.portaldaliteratura.com/entrevistas.php?id=17.

Kaës, R. (1976). *L'Appareil psychique groupal* [The psychic apparatus of the group]. Paris: Dunod.

Kaës, R. (1989). El pacto denegativo en los conjuntos trans-subjetivos [The denying pact]. In: A. Missenard, J. Guillaumin, G. Rosolato, J. Kristeva, Y. Gutierrez, J.-J. Baranes, R. Moury, R. Roussillon, R. Kaës (Eds.), *Lo Negativo.* Buenos Aires, Amorrortu.

Kaës, R. (1993). *Le groupe et le sujet du groupe* [The Group and the Group Subject]. Paris: Dunod.

Kaës, R. (1998a). Preface. In: R. Kaës, H. Faimberg, M. Enriquez, & J. J. Baranes (Eds.), *A transmissão do psiquismo entre as gerações* [The Transmission of Psychic Life across Generations] (pp. 5–19). Sao Paulo: Unimarco.

Kaës, R. (1998b). Os dispositivos psicanalíticos e as incidências da geração. In: R. Kaës, H. Faimberg, M. Enriquez, & J. J. Baranes (Eds.), *A transmissão do psiquismo entre gerações* [The transmission of psychic life across generations]. São Paulo: Unimarco.

Kaës, R., Faimberg, H., Enriquez, M., & Baranes, J. J. (Eds.) (1993). El sujeto de herencia [The Subject of Inheritance]. In: *Transmisión de la vida psíquica entre generaciones* [The Transmission of Psychic Life across Generations]. Paris: Dunod [reprinted Buenos Aires: Amorrortu, 1996].

Kancyper, L. (2006). *Resentimiento y remordimiento* [Resentment and Remorse]. Buenos Aires: Lumen.

Kinston, W. (1983). A theoretical context for shame. *International Journal of Psychoanalysis, 64*(2): 213–226.

Kitayama, O., & Matuki, K. (Eds.) (2004). *Japanese Contributions to Psychoanalysis.* Tokyo: Japan Psychoanalytical Society.

Klein, M. (1946). Notes on some schizoid mechanisms. *International Journal of Psychoanalysis, 27*: 99–110.

Lacan, J. (1964–1965). *The Four Fundamental Concepts of Psychoanalysis.* New York: W. W. Norton, 1998.

Lacan, J. (1972). *Encore, 21/11*. Paidos, Buenos Aires.

Lagache, D. (1951). Quelques aspects du transfert [Some aspects of transference]. *Revue française de psychoanalyse, 15*(3): 407–424.

Lagache, D. (1952). La theorie du transfert [The theory of transference]. *Revue française de psychoanalyse, 16*(1–2): 1–115.

Lagache, D. (1958). La psychanalyse et la structure de la personnalité [Psychoanalysis and personality structure]. In: *La Psychanalyse*. Paris: PUF.

Laing, R. D. (1961). *Self and Others*. London, Penguin, 1969.

Laing, R. D., & Esterson, A. (1967). *Sanity, Madness, and the Family: Families of Schizophrenics*. London, Penguin, 1970.

Laing, R. D., Phillipson, H., & Lee, A. R. (1966). *Interpersonal Perception: A Theory and a Method of Research*. London: Tavistock.

Langer, L. L. (1999). *Holocaust Testimonies: The Ruins of Memory*. New Haven, CT: Yale University Press.

Langer, M. (1981). *Memoria, historia y diálogo psicoanalítico* [Memory, History, and Psychoanalytic Dialogue]. Mexico DF: Folios.

Laplanche, J. (1987). *Problematiques V. Le baquet-trascendence du transfert*. Paris: PUF.

Laplanche, J., & Pontalis, J.-B. (1973). *The Language of Psychoanalysis*. London: Hogarth Press.

Lara, M. P. (2007). *Narrating Evil: A Postmetaphysical Theory of Reflective Judgment*. New York: Columbia University Press

Lazare, A. (2004). *On Apology*. Cambridge: Oxford University Press.

Levi, P. (1965). *The Truce: A Survivor's Journey Home from Auschwitz*. London: Bodley Head.

Levi, P. (1989). *The Drowned and the Saved*. New York, Vintage.

Lewis, H. B. (1971). *Shame and Guilt in Neurosis*. New York: International Universities Press.

Lidz, T., Cornelison, A., Fleck, S., & Terry, D. (1957). The interfamilial environment of the schizophrenic patient I: The father. *Psychiatry, 20*: 329–342.

Lindner, E. G. (2001). Humiliation and the human condition: mapping a minefield. *Human Rights Review, 2*(2): 46–63.

Lindner, E. G. (2006). *Making Enemies: Humiliation and International Conflict*. New York: Praeger.

Littell, J. (2007). *The Kindly Ones*. New York, Harper, 2009.

Losso, R. (2001). *Psicoanàlisis de la familia: Recorridos teórico-clìnicos* [Psychoanalysis of the Family: Theoretical and Clinical Pathways]. Buenos Aires: Lumen.

Malcolm, N. (1996). *Bosnia: A Short Story.* New York: New York University Press.

Margalit, A. (2002). *The Ethics of Memory.* Cambridge, MA: Harvard University Press.

Mead, G. H. (1982). *The Individual and the Social Self: Unpublished Essays by G. H. Mead,* D. L. Miller (Ed.). Chicago, IL: University of Chicago Press.

Merea, C. (2005). *Familia, Psicoanálisis y sociedad* [Family, Psychoanalysis, and Society]. Buenos Aires: Fondo de Cultura Económica.

Miller, W. I. (1993). *Humiliation and Other Essays on Honor, Social Discomfort and Violence.* Ithaca, NY: Cornell University Press

Mitchell, M. (1936). *Gone with the Wind.* New York: Macmillan.

Moguillansky, R. (2003). *Pensamiento único y diálogo cotidiano* [Unique thought and daily dialogue]. Buenos Aires: El Zorzal.

Moguillansky, R. (2004). *Nostalgia del Absoluto, extrañeza y perplejidad* [Longing for the absolute, strangenes and perplexity]. Buenos Aires: El Zorzal.

Moguillansky, R., & Szpilka, J. (2009). *Crítica de la Razón Natural* [Critique of Natural Reason]. Buenos Aires: Biebel.

Money-Kyrle, R. (1961). *The Construction of Our World Model, in Man´s Picture of His World.* London: Duckworth.

Morrison, A. P. (1989). *Shame: The Underside of Narcissism.* Hillsdale, NJ: Analytic Press.

Nachin, C. (1995). *El psiquismo ante la prueba de las generaciones* [The Psyche Before the Test of Generations]. Buenos Aires: Amorrortu, 1997.

Nasio, J. D. (2012). *Commeny agir avec un adolescent en crise* [How To Deal with an Adolescent in Crisis]. Paris, Payot.

Nell, V. (2006). Cruelty's reward: the gratifications of perpetrators and spectators. *Behavioral and Brain Sciences, 29*: 211–257.

Nichols, M., & Schwartz, R. (2007). *The Essentials of Family Therapy.* Boston, MA: Pearson, Allyn & Bacon.

Nicola, U. (2005). *Filosofia.* [Philosophy]. Rio de Janeiro: Globo.

Norris, C. (2007). *Truth, Knowledge, and the Credo of Rumsfield.* London: Continuum Books.

Pfeiffer, E. (Ed.) (1985). *Sigmund Freud and Lou Andreas-Salome, Letters.* New York: W. W. Norton.

Plomin, R., & Caspi, A. (1998). DNA and personality. *European Journal of Personality, 12*: 387–407.

Pontalis, J.-B. (1963). Le petit groupe comme objet [The small group as object]. In: *Après Freud.* Paris: Julliard, 1965; Gallimard, 1968.

Preston, S. D., Bechara, A., Grabowski, T. J., Damasio, H., & Damasio, A. R. (2007). The neural substrates of cognitive empathy. *Social Neuroscience, 2*(3–4), 254–275.

Puchades, R. (2005). Ideas para una metasicología de la vergüenza [Ideas for a metapsychology of shame]. *Revista de Psicoanálisis de la A. P. de Madrid*, 45: 119–134.

Puget, J., & Berenstein, I. (1998). *Psicoanálisis de la pereja matrimonial*. [Psychoanalysis of the Marital Couple]. Buenos Aires: Paidós.

Puget, J., de Bianchedi, E. T., Bianchedi, M., Braun, J., & Pelento, M. L. (1993). Violencia social transgresora. *Gaceta Psicológica*, 94: 11–23.

Reiss, D., Plomin, R., Neiderhiser, J. M., & Heathrington, E. M. (2003). *The Relationship Code: Deciphering Genetic and Social Influences on Adolescent Development* . Cambridge, MA: Harvard University Press.

Ricoeur, P. (1995). *Le pardon peut-il guérir?* [Can Forgiveness Bring Healing?]. Paris: Espirit, Revue Internationale.

Rivera, A. (1993). *La revolución es un sueño eterno* [The Revolution is an Eternal Dream]. Buenos Aires: Alfaguara.

Romero, J. L. (1987). *Estudio de la mentalidad burguesa*, [Studies of the Bourgeois Mentality]. Buenos Aires: Alianza, 2006.

Rosenthal, R., & Jacobson, L. (1992). *Pygmalion in the Classroom: Teacher Expectation and Pupils' Intellectual Development*. New York: Irving.

Rousillon, R. (1985). *Paradoxes et situations limites de la psychanalyse*. Paris: PUF (1991).

Ruffiot, A., Eiguer, A., Litovsky, D. Gear, M. C., Liendo, E. C., & Perrot, J. (1981). *La Thérapie Familiale Psychanalytique* [Psychoanalytic Family Therapy]. Paris: Dunod.

Russell, B. (1914). The relation of sense-data to physics. *Scientia*, 4. Republished in *Mysticism and Logic*. London: Unwin Books, 1917.

Rycroft, C. (1968). *A Critical Dictionary of Psychoanalysis*. London: Thomas Nelson.

Santayana, G. (1905). *Reasons in Common Sense: The Life of Reason*, vol 1. Mineola, NY: Dover, 1980.

Sartre, J.-P. (1952). *Saint Genet, Comedian and Actor*. Minneapolis, MN: University of Minnesota Press, 2012.

Sartre, J.-P. (1960). *Critique of Dialectic Reason*. New York: Verso Books, 2006.

Scheff, T. (1999). *Being Mentally Ill: A Sociological Theory*. 3a. Edition. New York: Aldine de Gruyter.

Scheff, T. (2000). *Bloody Revenge: Emotions, Nationalism and War*. Lincoln, NE: i.universe.com

Scheff, T. J. (2004). Thoughts in response to *Blind Trust* (2004), by V. Volkan, a theory of collective violence. Accessed at: www.humiliation studies.org/news-old/archives/000168.html.

Scheff, T., & Retzinger, S. M. (1991a). *Emotions and Violence: Shame and Rage in Destructive Conflicts*. Lexington, MA: Lexington Books.

Scheff, T., & Retzinger, S. M. (1991b). *Violent Emotions: Shame and Rage in Marital Quarrels*. Thousand Oaks, CA: Sage.

Scheff, T., & Retzinger, S. (2000). Shame as a master emotion of everyday life. *Journal of Mundane Behavior, 1*(3). Accessed at www.mundanebehavior.org/issues/v1n3/scheff-retzinger.htm.

Seligman, M. P. (1975). *Helplessness: On Depression, Development, and Death*. San Francisco, CA: Freeman.

Selvini Palazzoli, M., Boscolo, L., Cecchin, G. F., & Prata, G. (1974). *Paradox and Counterparadox*. New York: Jason Aronson, 1978.

Shapiro, D. (2003). The tortured, not the torturer, are ashamed. *Social Research, 70*(4): 1148.

Sluzki, C. E. (1993). Toward a general model of family and political victimization. *Psychiatry, 56*: 178–187.

Sluzki, C. E. (2004). House invaded by ghosts: culture, migration and development in a Moroccan family invaded by hallucinations. *Families, Systems and Health, 22*(3): 321–337.

Sluzki, C. E. (2006). Victimización, recuperación y las historias "con mejor forma" [Victimization, recovery, and the "better formed" stories]. *Sistemas Familiares, 22*(1): 5–20.

Sluzki, C. E. (2007). Lyman C. Wynne and the transformation of the field of family-and-schizophrenia. *Family Process, 46*(2): 143–149.

Sluzki, C. E. (2010). The pathway between conflict and reconciliation: coexistence as an evolutionary process. *Transcultural Psychiatry, 47*(1): 55–69.

Sluzki, C. E., & Ransom, D. (1976). *Double-Bind: The Foundation of the Communicational Approach to the Family*. New York: Grune & Stratton.

Sluzki, C. E., Berenstein, I., Bleichmar, H., & Maldonado Allende, I. (Eds.) (1970). *Patología y terapéutica del grupo familiar* [Pathology and therapeutics of the family group]. Buenos Aires: ACTA.

Sontag, S. (2003). *Regarding the Pain of Others*. New York: Farrar, Straus and Giroux.

Spivacow, M. A. (2005). La intervención vincular en el tratamiento psico-analítico de pareja. *Aperturas Psicoanalíticas, 19*. Accessed at: www.aperturas.org.

Steinberg, B. (1991). Psychoanalytic concepts in international politics: the role of shame and humiliation. *International Review of Psycho-Analysis, 18*: 65–85.

Steiner, G. (1974). *Nostalgia for the Absolute*. Toronto, ON: House of Anansi Press.

Tienari, P., Wynne, L. C., & Wahlberg, K.-E. (2006). Genetics and family relationships in schizophrenia and the schizophrenia spectrum disorders. In: S. M. Miller, S. McDaniel, J. Rolland, & S. Feetham (Eds.), *Individuals, Families, and the New Era of Genetics: Biopsychosocial Perspectives* (pp. 445–464). New York: Norton.

Tienari, P., Wynne, L. C., Moring, J., Lahti, I. Naarala, M. Sorri, A., Wahlberg, K, E. Saarento, O., Seitamaa, M., Kaleva, M., et al. (1994). The Finnish adoptive family study of schizophrenia: implications for family research. *British Journal of Psychiatry, 164*(suppl. 23): 20–26.

Tienari, P., Wynne, L. C., Sorri, A., Lahti, I., Laksy, K., Moring, J., Naarala, M. Nieminen, P., & Wahlberg, K.-E. (2004). Genotype-environment interaction in schizophrenia-spectrum disorder. Long-term follow-up study of Finnish adoptees. *British Journal of Psychiatry, 184*: 216–222.

Velasco, R. (2002). El sentimiento de si y el afecto de vergüenza Intersubjetivo [The experience of self and the emotion of intersubjective shame]. *Rev. de Psicoterapia Psicoanalítica y Salud, 4*(2): 287–294.

Visacovsky, S. (2002). *El Lanús: Memoria, política y psicoanálisis en la Argentina (1956–1992)* [The Lanús: Memory, Politics, and Psychoanalysis in Argentina 1956–1992]. Buenos Aires: Alianza,

Volkan, V. (2004). *Blind Trust: Large Groups and their Leaders in Times of Crisis and Terror.* Charlottesville, VA: Pitchstone.

Von Foerster, H. (2002). Vision, language and knowledge: the double blind. In: D. F. Schnitman & J. Schnitman (Eds.), *New Paradigms, Culture and Subjectivity* (pp. 65–81). Cresskill, NJ: Hamptom Press.

Wahlberg, K.-E., Wynne, L. C., Hakko, H., Laksy, K., Moring, J., Miettunen, J., & Tienari, P. (2004). Interaction of genetic risk and adoptive parent communication deviance: longitudinal prediction of adoptee psychiatric disorders. *Psychological Medicine, 34*(8): 1531–1541.

Watzlawick, P., Beavin, J. H., & Jackson, D. D. (1967). *Pragmatics of Human Communication: A Study of Interactional Patterns, Pathologies, and Paradoxes.* New York: W. W. Norton.

Whitman, W. (2008). *Leaves of Grass.* Radford, VA: Wilder.

Willi, J. (1976). *La pareja humana: relación y conflict* [The Human Couple: Relationship and Conflict]. Buenos Aires: Morata.

Willi, J. (2004). *Psychologie der Liebe.* Stuttgart: Klett-Cotta

Winnicott, D. W. (1971). *Playing and Reality.* London: Tavistock.

Wittgenstein, L. (1922). *Tractatus Logico-Philosophicus.* London: Kegan Paul, Trench, Trubner.

Wolfson, M. (2009). *Mauricio Goldenberg.* Buenos Aires: CI Capital Intelectual.

Wynne, L. C., Ryckoff, I. M., Day, J., & Hirsch, S. I. (1958). Pseudo-mutu-ality in the family relations of schizophrenics. *Psychiatry, 21*: 205–220.

Wynne, L. C., Tienari, P., Nieminen, P., Sorri, A., Latí, I., Moring, J., Naarala, M., Laksy, K., Wahlberg, K.-E., & Miettunen, J. (2006a). I. Genotype-environment interaction in the schizophrenia spectrum: genetic liability and global family ratings in the Finnish adoption study. *Family Process, 45*(4): 419–434.

Wynne, L. C., Tienari, P., Sorri, A., Lahti, I., Moring, J., & Wahlberg K.-E. (2006b). II. Genotype-environment interaction in the schizophrenia spectrum: qualitative observations. *Family Process, 45*(4): 435–447.

INDEX